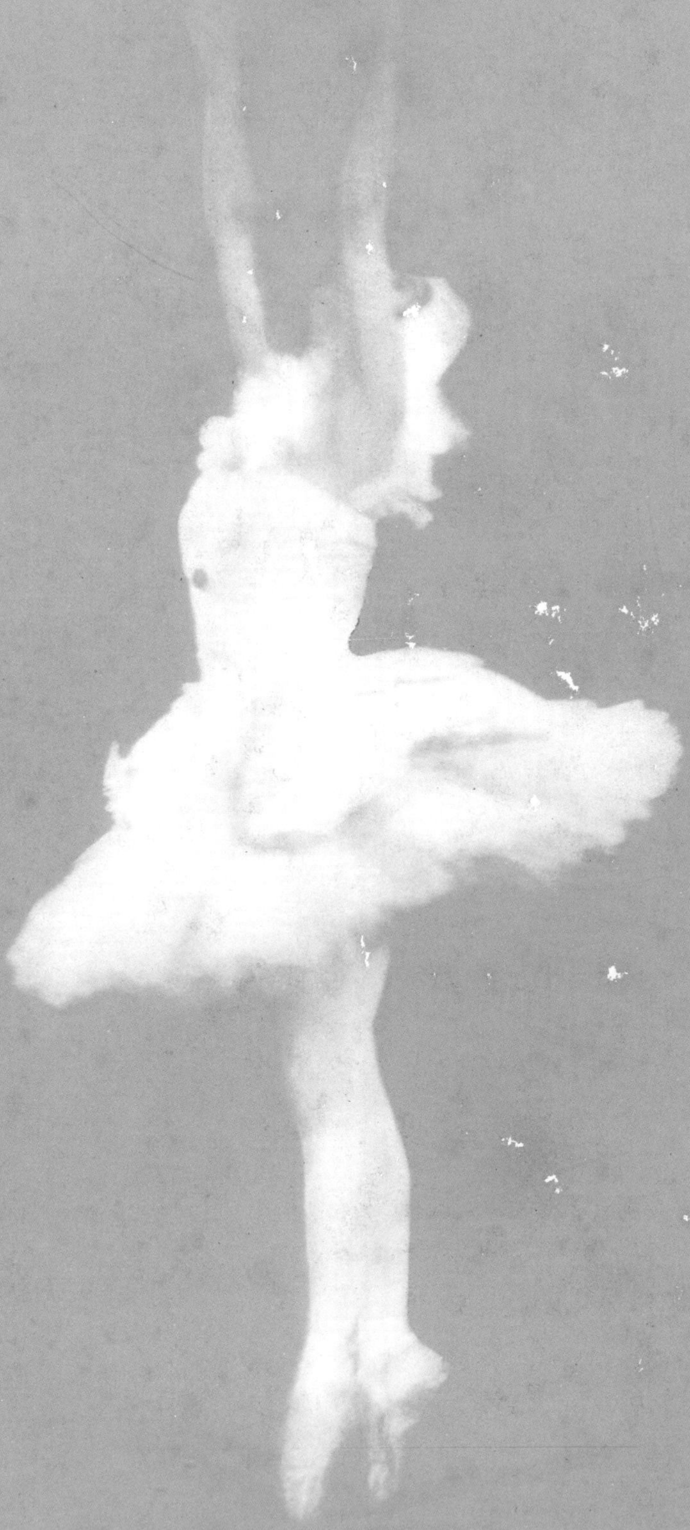

PAVLOVA

IMPRESSIONS

PAVLOVA

IMPRESSIONS

PRESENTED BY

MARGOT FONTEYN

WEIDENFELD AND NICOLSON · LONDON

First published in Great Britain in 1984
by George Weidenfeld & Nicolson Limited
91 Clapham High Street, London sw4

ISBN 0 297 78454 4

Editors: Roberta and John Lazzarini

House editor: Felicity Luard

Designer: Simon Bell

Text set by Keyspools Ltd, Golborne, Lancs
Printed and bound in Italy by L.E.G.O. Vicenza

Frontispiece: *Christmas*

Opposite: Pavlova in 1909. Drawing by Valentin Serov

Page 8: *The Dying Swan*

Page 10: Pavlova *c.* 1900, St Petersburg

To the wonderful dancers of today
who are so magnificently fulfilling
the hopes and visions of
ANNA PAVLOVA

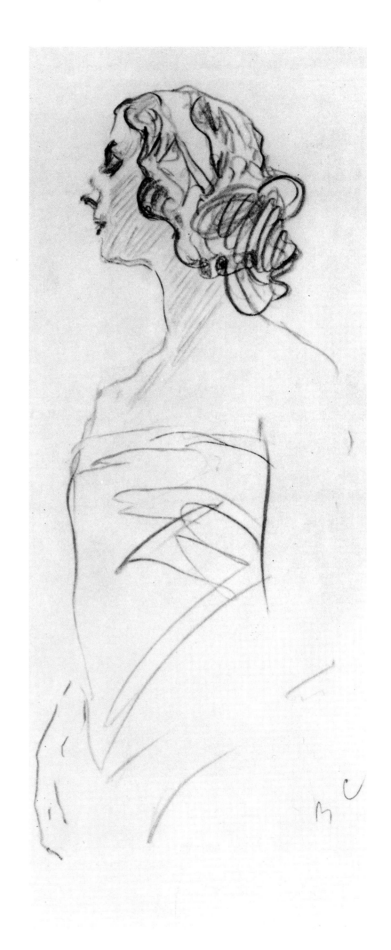

CONTENTS

ANNA PAVLOVA *by Sir Frederick Ashton*

Page 9

INTRODUCTION *by Margot Fonteyn*

Page 11

I

Page 13

The Russian Ballet — *Revelation* — *The Imperial Ballet School* — *Graduation* — *Early Influences*
Giselle — *Enrico Cecchetti* — *A Dancer's Day* — *First Tour* — *King Oscar*
King Edward — *A St Petersburg Interview* — *New York* — *London*

II

Page 49

An Art New to America — *Interview in Indiana* — *Ballet Shoes* — *The Quarrel*
Dancing with Nijinsky — *Glamour* — *Shopping for Chic* — *Ivy House* — *A Ballerina's Home*
Pavlova's Swans — *Soul of a Slav* — *Pride of St Petersburg* — *The Volcano*
A Renunciation — *Last Performance in Russia* — *Premonition*

III

Page 85

The War Years — *The Dumb Girl of Portici* — *Opera and Ballet*
The Big Show — *An Enigma* — *All Havana Dancing* — *Mexico*
Touring Latin America — *After the War* — *Looking to the East* — *Japan*
Russian Ballet in Tokyo — *India* — *Ajanta Frescoes* — *East and West*

IV

Page 119

The Incomparable — *Genius* — *The Spirit of America* — *The Jazz* — *Why She Danced It*
Brighter Londoners — *A Sacred Ritual* — *Reality and Dream* — *Australia* — *Visions Fulfilled*
The Old Order — *The Wide World* — *The Swan* — *Immortal Pavlova*

SELECTIVE CHRONOLOGY 152 — BALLETS ILLUSTRATED 154

PHOTOGRAPHIC ACKNOWLEDGMENTS 154

SOURCE REFERENCES 155 — INDEX 158

'I do not think in words. My medium of expression is movement.'

ANNA PAVLOVA

by Sir Frederick Ashton

Without question Anna Pavlova was the greatest theatrical genius that I have ever seen. Her personality was of such power and vibrancy that on her first entrance on to the stage she sent an electric shock throughout the audience.

Her grace and poise I have never seen equalled in any dancer. She was, however, a law unto herself. There have been many dancers who were technically more proficient but what she attempted to do within her means was inimitable. Nevertheless she had certain technical feats within her command which I have never seen bettered.

With the exception of *Giselle*, in which she gave a great performance, I never saw her attempt the big classical role, but often, with the most trivial theme and the most trite music, she would create epics of life and death and of what living means. Her plasticity of movement was unique and she was alive in every aspect of her fragile and delicate body. With this glorious instrument she could convey every nuance of feeling from passion to deep melancholy. All this was made easy for her by her sensitive and expressive feet, and by the use she made of her wonderful hands with which she could stir the human soul to great depths.

No audience was ever indifferent to her, she stirred them and often even made them feel uneasy. The male element of an audience often found her positive features too potent, which rebelled against their ideas of femininity. Her most fervant devotees were the female element of the audience, but anybody who saw her to this day still retains a clear vision of this translucent being.

In a sense she was a great missionary for she travelled the entire world in those difficult days before the aeroplane, and she would appear under circumstances which would baulk many a dancer today. I first saw her in Lima, Peru, as a small boy, and I immediately became infected by her. From that moment I never wished to do anything else but be connected with the dance. At the other end of the world in Australia she did the same to Robert Helpmann, and to countless others wherever she appeared.

What is extraordinary is that though many of her greatest dance images were mere fragments, and often seemed like improvisations round a theme, yet more emotion was distilled into these items than one might get from a complete ballet. Her curtain calls were in themselves performances of outstanding beauty, often taking longer than the dance she had just executed, for she ravished and enchanted her audience with each separate entrance that she made. This resulted in the most telling poems of movement that one can ever imagine, and it seemed that the public was reluctant to ever let this exclusive spirit flee from its grasp.

Of her epoch she was undoubtedly the most famous name throughout the world. Her name can never die, and such a living and passionate spirit must continue to haunt the world to which she gave so much delight and inspiration.

INTRODUCTION

by Margot Fonteyn

'When what Pavlova said is hidden in musty old newspaper files, the remembrance of how she said it will remain in the memory of the interviewer. ... Her smile has in it the charm of a summer morning, when all the world is gay and birds make melody in mid-air. She talks with an animation in the manner, an enthusiasm in the matter, that are all too rare in a blasé world of mostly commonplace folk.'

These words were written in 1917. I found them when reading through three albums of press cuttings that once belonged to Anna Pavlova. These unique albums had come up for sale at Sotheby's as items in the vast ballet collection of my old friend John Carr Doughty, a businessman and balletomane such as Pavlova might have known in her St Petersburg days. My collaborators, Roberta and John Lazzarini, acquired them for the Pavlova Society and the Museum in London of which they are the curators.

The Lazzarini's felt the press cuttings should be preserved in a more permanent form, and when they approached me I was immediately filled with enthusiasm.

During our work on the book we experienced a growing revelation of Pavlova's personality. We were fascinated by her lively mind, her professionalism, her energy, her enduring idealism. At the same time we were saddened by the strange fate that brought her so few rewards for the incalculable gift of beauty she gave the world.

We have tried to show the gradual transformation from eager child, through dedicated student, fledgling ballerina, excited young celebrity, to supreme artist, mature woman and eventually to the pure essence of dance.

In attempting to illuminate Pavlova's magical personality we have drawn first on her spoken word in interviews and the written words attributed to her in articles, bearing in mind that the latter have been edited and sometimes translated at least once. For that reason I have selected with very great care only those words which ring true to my ear, knowing, as I do, something of what it means to dance year in and year out, trying always to find within oneself that fresh inspiration which alone brings truth and spontaneity to the performance.

To give depth to our portrait, we have also included observations from the memoirs of Victor Dandré, Theodore Stier and André Olivéroff, among others, who worked closely with Pavlova.

The nature of the material meant that we often had to abridge ruthlessly and, sometimes, in the interests of the narrative, sections from different articles have been amalgamated (indicated by an asterisk), but never have we altered the sense of what was said.

We the collaborators, wish to thank most warmly for their help in various ways Dr Angelita Legarda, Lesley Clifford, Asya Chorley, Kate Regan, Kenji Usui, Mariko Yukawa, Dr and Mrs Harmodio Arias and Dr and Mrs Gilberto Arias – and Sir Frederick Ashton for his eloquent description of Pavlova. We express our deepest appreciation to our editor Felicity Luard and our designer Simon Bell, of Weidenfeld, for their tireless efforts throughout the making of this book.

It is our particular hope that Pavlova's home, Ivy House in London, will one day be restored and preserved as a museum and a centre for activities concerned with young dancers. I am sure there is nothing Pavlova would have wanted more. As a first step, one third of the proceeds from this book will go to a fund devoted to that purpose. It is called the Pavlova Appeal.

I

A gleam! a flash! a shimmering vision of beauty! Light, as of the sun caught and reflected by wings of gauze. White limbs that move like light itself.

Is it some creature from fairyland, some spirit of ethereal grace freed from the terrestrial trammels of the flesh? Is it some magical embodiment of the music of movement conjured up by man's imagination?

No. Merely Pavlova, the incomparable Pavlova.

Those words came from the Manchester Evening News; *the year was 1925.*

Now consider that Anna Pavlova was forty-four with seventeen years of hard touring, long journeys, professional difficulties of every kind behind her, and that Manchester was a city layered over with years of grime which made black mud in the streets when it rained – as it does frequently in England. And imagine that Pavlova, in the middle of a not very inspiring provincial tour, came out on to the stage one night and was able to arouse that flight of poetic exaltation in the heart of that writer. Don't think it is easy or normal for even a great artist to do that; only one whose whole life was a quest for truth and beauty.

You can be very sure that few mortals have, or ever have had, the mysterious, magical power of Pavlova, the 'Incomparable' – as she was so justifiably called.

How did Pavlova become – Pavlova?

I learned my art under as nearly perfect conditions as are ever found on this earth. The Russian ballet owes its subtle perfection of detail, its greatness, its rank to the fact that it is made up of dancers who from the day they went to live in the dormitories of the Imperial School saw nothing – were surrounded by nothing – but beauty – beauty! – and the highest standards physically, mentally, morally and spiritually.

From the very hour that my mother gave me into the keeping of the Imperial School to the time I began my world wanderings I never saw a badly painted, cheap or stupid picture; I never read an ill-written, tawdry or trashy book; I never saw acting that was not of the finest; I never attended an ill-made play or a badly sung opera; I never ate a badly cooked or ill-chosen meal; I never slept in a poorly ventilated room; I neither worked nor played too long; I never witnessed gross manners. ... My general education, from mathematics and languages to science, came to me from the finest teachers procurable. The special training in dancing was in the hands of Marius Petipa and his associates.

And to Marius Petipa and the Imperial School I make grateful obeisance that I am – Pavlova.

These words have such a clear, clean aura of truth that I feel they are an important key to the woman and artist I hold above all others in the long history of ballet.

After all, from what does an artist create his art if not from things seen, heard, taught and experienced, and from his moral and spiritual beliefs?

Anna Pavlova was perhaps more than usually sensitive to the artistic qualities surrounding her in her developing years, and to the inspiration she gained from contact with theatre artists of the highest calibre in the setting of one of the most beautiful cities in the world.

Opposite The schoolgirl. *Below* Theatre Street, St Petersburg. The ballet school occupies the building on the right-hand side.

I was born in St Petersburg. I learned to dance in the ballet school in St Petersburg and I danced in the Maryinsky Theatre in St Petersburg.⋆

My first memories go back to the time when I lived with my mother in a little apartment. I was the only child and we two were alone in the world; my father died when I was two.

My mother was very pious; she taught me to make the sign of the cross and to recite my prayers before the holy icon in our little living room. . . .

We were very poor but nevertheless my mother always found the means to provide me with an unexpected treat on holidays. At Easter some toys hidden in my huge Easter egg and at Christmas we always had our little fir tree decorated with gilded fruits and glittering in the light of candles.⋆

Until I was eight I never dreamed what dancing could mean. My mother saved up enough money to buy us tickets for the upper balcony at the Maryinsky Theatre. I'd never before been to a theatre.⋆

When we set out for the Maryinsky the snow that had just fallen glistened in the reflection of the street lights, and our sleigh slid noiselessly over the frozen streets. Seated beside my mother, her arm around my waist, I was suffused with happiness.

'You are going to see the country of the fairies,' she said as we were drawn rapidly through the night toward the unknown, mysterious thing which was the theatre.⋆

The ballet was the *Sleeping Beauty* with Tchaikovsky's enchanting music. From the first measures of the orchestra I became very grave and began to tremble, troubled for the first time by the thrill of the beautiful.

Pavlova, who was a seven-month baby, was a highly strung, sensitive child. The seed of her artistry must have been born within her, but her words here make one believe that it was touched by the light on that winter evening, as she sat in the great blue and gold decorated auditorium which she herself would one day fill with cheering, ardent admirers.

Opposite 'My earliest memories are of my mother, a frail, gentle-faced lady, carrying on an untiring struggle against poverty.'
Below The Maryinsky Theatre.

There exist several versions of Pavlova's first experience of ballet, and in fact I have drawn on more than one. I love the telling details of the sleigh ride to the theatre in awed anticipation of she-knew-not-what, and her troubled emotion on encountering, for the first time, the inexplicable beauty of music and theatre.

St Petersburg itself must have looked like a fairy tale in the glistening snow, and the little girl's eyes must have been as large as soup plates, and shining with excitement all evening.

Later her eyes would impress and hold the attention of everyone who went to interview her. 'The intense nature of the great Russian dancer ... with her dark expressive eyes, like pools of black ink, veiled in mystery, the great mystery of the unknown ...' was how one writer remembered her after her death.

From that night on I knew I must give the rest of my life to dancing. I was a frail child, weakened by under-nourishment .... A dozen people told me I could not stand the long, hard training of ballet school. They did not know how my longing would give me strength. I gave my mother no rest until one blessed morning she led me to the school and entered my application. They told me to come back when I was ten.

I spent the next two years in constant imitation of what I had seen that one night. I prayed over and over the school would accept me.

On my tenth birthday I went back, hoping, hoping. The examinations were very strict. Many times those in charge doubtfully shook their heads. But they must have heard the prayer that was in my heart all the time. They took me in.

Opposite The earliest known photograph of Pavlova dressed for class.

Below A classroom in the ballet school.

My poor mother did not want me to be a dancer. It was only when, after my hard training, I received the title of prima ballerina, that my mother was satisfied.★

Of all the ballet schools in the world today there is none so strict as that of the Maryinsky Theatre in St Petersburg. It is far more exacting ... than the ballet school of the opera house in Paris.

Little boys and girls are selected to study the art of the ballet when they are only nine [or ten].★

The little children on these occasions are dressed up in their best finery, and it is usual to have a gathering of about 500 people, out of whom 250 will be children. ... At the top of the hall there is a large, round table ... at which there sit the ballet-masters and the high directors of the ballet institute.

Each child is brought before them, and requested to walk up and down, and go through various exercises to show whether the body is lithe, supple, and suitable for dancing.★

If her legs and arms present the requisite symmetry and if she walks, skips, and runs with evidence of natural grace the child is qualified on the first essentials.★

Those who are considered suitable have to go to another room, to be examined by a doctor to see if they are physically in good health. The number passed by the doctor's examination is subsequently reduced by selection, and although one year as many as fifteen were selected, it is not usual to choose more than twelve. The selected children are placed under special tuition. ...

In a year's time they go through an examination, and if they have improved and ... are likely to become efficient ballet dancers, they are taken inside the institute.★

Unless the child happens to live near enough to the school to be brought there before half past eight in the morning, she takes up her residence in the school for a term of nine months in every year of her stay there.★

When we first go there we are not only taught the exercises in the ballet; we must also go through the regular education that children of our years would be expected to acquire. We learn to play the piano and something about acting and pantomime [and] we see the poses of famous statues. We are all put into blue uniforms like the other school children of Russia.★

Dining room in the Imperial Ballet School.

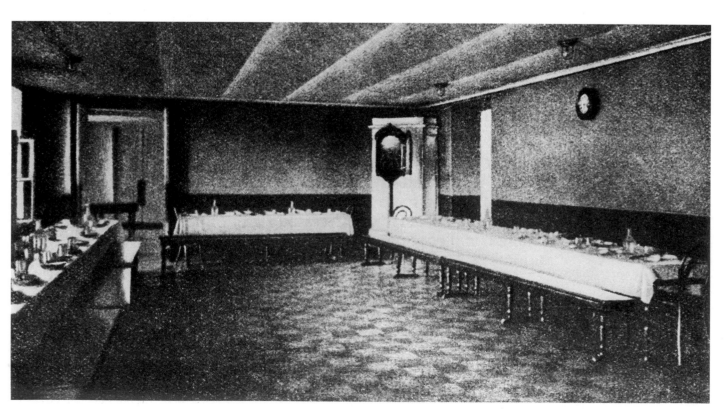

We fortunate inmates ... received the finest medical attention. No child was permitted to get up on the toes until it was known that [her] little ankles and legs were strong enough and ready.

After I had been in the Imperial Conservatory about two years I began to be used in such ballets or operas that required children.

One of the tremendous events in my life at this time was when I assumed the role of a lotus bud at a most elaborate entertainment given by the Tsar in honour of the Kaiser at Peterhof, the royal palace outside St Petersburg.*

It was not owing to any particular merit of my own that I came in contact with the Russian Court. ... I shared this distinction with all the other little girls who are trained in the Imperial Ballet School. There was a dear little theatre with a low stage upon which the pupils gave a performance once every year.

The Emperor Alexander III never missed these representations, which were always followed by a festive supper. The members of the Imperial family sat in the midst of the girls, who were taught to use their knives and forks gracefully for these occasions.

These gatherings were not a little awe-inspiring. At one of them the Emperor Alexander III took my little friend Stanislava in his arms and kissed her as a reward for her performance of a particularly difficult step. That was a sad day for me. I shed bitter tears of jealousy and stamped my feet. To console me, the Grand Duke Vladimir let me ride on his knee! But still my grief knew no bounds, as I said that the Emperor ought also to have taken me in his arms and kissed me!*

When any performances are going to be given at the Tsar's residence in St Petersburg, it is customary for ballerinas to attend there, but the Emperor, before I had reached this position, commanded me one day to take part in a little ballet. ...

The Emperor's keenness for the ballet was so great that ... he never missed attending a Sunday performance. (I should have explained that the ballets are given every Sunday and Wednesday.)*

Often the Tsar, after a performance, will come on the stage and personally compliment any members of the ballet whose work he thinks calls for congratulations. He is always very kind in that way.

A dormitory in the Imperial Ballet School.

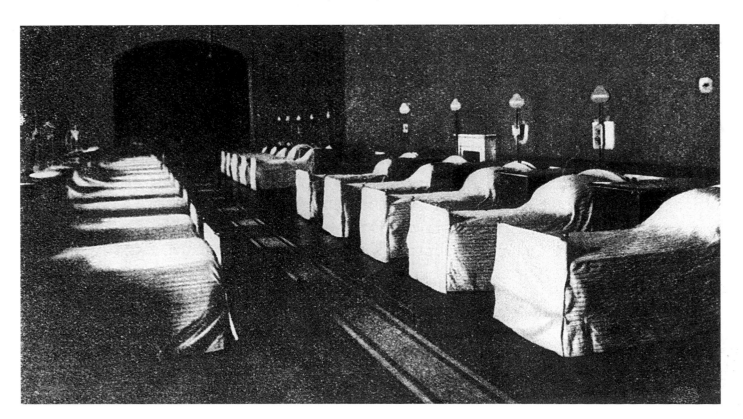

Six months before her graduation Pavlova appeared in what is counted as her official debut on the stage of the Maryinsky Theatre in a pas de trois *in* Daughter of the Pharaoh. *Critic Alexander Pleshcheyev wrote these very perceptive words: 'The little Pavlova, with her fragile-looking knees, charmed everybody with her femininity, lightness and grace.' Those adjectives were to follow her throughout her life as countless writers tried to describe her rare quality of movement. She herself always loved to talk of the school to which she attributed her success.*

There is a belief among some people that the quality, the excellence of Russian dancing is due to the fact that it is Russian; that only to the Russian is given the true genius of the dance. I am often asked to confirm this opinion. And that, of course, is impossible. . . .

In truth, the Imperial School as it was founded . . . was a French school housed in Russia. But French it did not remain. The Russian temperament quickly absorbed the Latin, nationalized it, coloured it with the Slavic emotionalism, until in the end . . . the school was uniquely and completely Russian.

Just as Pavlova explains how French training and style were made uniquely Russian, so, today, one can see how Russian training and style have been made uniquely American in the United States by George Balanchine, himself a product of the Imperial School that produced Pavlova. So it is that classical ballet technique evolves while remaining basically unchanged.

Upon the completion of the allotted . . . years of my study I became, automatically, a member of the Imperial Ballet.

Like an army, the Imperial Ballet had its rank and file and its leaders. At first one was merely among the *corps de ballet* present. One was a leaf or a bud or a flower petal fluttering or swaying or drifting about the stage with dozens of one's kind, as the occasion demanded.

Then, if one fluttered or swayed or drifted diligently enough, the Tsar, at the recommendation of the director of the Imperial Theatre, promoted one from the ranks. The ecstasy of that moment when a dancer ceased to be atmosphere and became an individual! The feeling of delicious importance that dizzied one as one stepped forward from one's fellows to do one's special bit – for the first time!

Opposite The young artist. *Below* Graduation photograph, 1899. Pavlova is sitting on the extreme left.

Success is not only a matter of talent and hard work. It also requires being in the right place at the right time.

Pavlova appreciated how fortunate she was at the beginning of her career to be surrounded and helped by so many of the outstanding figures of the ballet world, a large number of whom happened to have been drawn into the orbit of St Petersburg. For example, her teachers, Johansson, Gerdt and Sokolova had been great artists in their own right, so she had the finest traditions of the past ingrained in her with every lesson at the school and later as a member of the company.

The Maryinsky Ballet was ruled for untold years by the great ballet-master and choreographer Marius Petipa, of whom Pavlova said, 'The genius Petipa took me under his wing during my first years on the stage.'

The leading ballerinas were Matilda Kchessinskaya, Olga Preobrajenskaya and the immensely popular Italian guest artist Pierina Legnani, all of them wonderful examples of the old school.

Then there was her own outstanding group of contemporaries, who would push classical ballet forward into the twentieth century: among them Vaslav Nijinsky, Tamara Karsavina and Michel Fokine – the pivotal choreographer between the old and the new. (V.P. Lappa, to whom she refers in the following quotation, was attached to the administrative staff.)

Two years after my debut, when I started to complain to V.P. Lappa I wasn't being given any chances, the dear man gave me a good talking to: 'You want to be a prima ballerina without putting any work into it? You want me to give you *La Bayadère*. What have you done to deserve it?'

His lengthy lecture came straight from the heart and I will always remember it. I realized then that first I would have to give something interesting and only then could I demand promotion. After the talk with Lappa, when I had pulled myself together, I began to study with E.P. Sokolova.

The press soon noticed my success. I danced the leading role in *The Awakening of Flora*, then in *The Magic Flute*. And then I got the part in *La Bayadère*. At first they wanted to try me out in The 'Shades' scene only. But I said I wanted to demonstrate a whole range of emotions – and they gave in! Then I was given *Giselle*. They didn't really have much trust in me, so I asked them to put on the ballet in the spring and promised to work all through Lent.

Opposite As Hoarfrost in *The Seasons*, 1900. This was the first role specially created for Pavlova.

Below Her first leading part, the title role in
The Awakening of Flora, 1900.

*The slightly younger ballerina Tamara Karsavina
explains why the directorate doubted Pavlova's technique
and stamina for the more taxing ballets.*

The ideal of Italian virtuosity reigned paramount on
our stage. Our dancers were judged by comparison
with Pierina Legnani, for many years the undisputed
star of the Maryinsky. Pavlova's figure, delicate, thin
almost to angularity, was in direct contradiction to
the muscular, steel-toed type of dancer then in vogue.
Pavlova was a throwback, a reincarnation of the
charm of an almost forgotten romanticism.

Very likely it was the instinct of her genius that
made her solicit the revival of that romantic master-
piece, *Giselle*. Giselle was the first serious part for
Pavlova, and it was understandable that the complete
grasp of dramatic situations came to her only with
time. But from the first she gave her interpretation a
pathos which could not have been surpassed. . . . That
pathos and the quality of incorporeal grace were
essential features of Pavlova's genius.

In *Giselle* Pavlova found herself and made her
public accept her unconditionally.

Opposite and right Pavlova as Giselle.

Below Silver-gilt wreath presented on her debut in *Giselle*, 1903.

Even though she had established herself with the role of Giselle, Pavlova was by no means a fully fledged artist – as she knew very well. She lost no opportunity to gain experience in other ballets; whatever came her way was a source of learning.

The happiest time for me is when I am working on a new role. I have been very fortunate that Petipa prepared me in my first roles, and I owe much to the advice of Sokolova and Cecchetti. I completely agree with them that it is impossible to learn a new ballet in a week: it takes at least six months. The comparison may seem a little gross, but an artist who is preparing a new role is rather like a pregnant woman. I become a much 'nicer' person, and because I am totally absorbed in my work, life seems so much sweeter.

I read the libretto with great care. I listen and relisten to the music. I seek the advice of the older ballerinas. And I try, both at home and at rehearsal, to dance and act in complete harmony, so that I am living in the world of my imagination around the clock.⋆

Giselle and *La Bayadère* are my *pièces de résistance*. Of course, I also dance other ballets. I appeared in *Le Corsaire*, then in *Paquita*, then *Don Quixote* and *Sleeping Beauty* – and in small ballets choreographed by Fokine. I can sense which ballet is good for me and which doesn't suit my talents. But I dance all these ballets to improve my repertoire.

It was not enough for Pavlova just to improve her repertoire. She still felt insecure in her technique.

Russian ballerinas sometimes went to Milan during their summer holidays for special coaching, because the Italian schooling was famous for developing strength and virtuosity.

Pavlova went even further by engaging the finest Italian teacher, Enrico Cecchetti, to give her private lessons in the studio of her St Petersburg home.

When Johansson, Gerdt and Sokolova told me there was nothing more to learn I went to Enrico Cecchetti. He found a weakness in the back and some fault with the hands. For three years I worked as never before, until he approved of my carriage. Of such things a dancer is made. But first you must have the will to drive yourself.

Opposite The bedroom of Pavlova's apartment, opening into the studio.

Below A private lesson with Cecchetti.

No matter how late I go to bed, I am always up by nine o'clock, for I must take my lesson with Cecchetti every day. Hardly have I gulped down a cup of tea before he is banging on the door with his cane and grumbling that I'm late.

My lesson with Cecchetti lasts two hours and is conducted according to the Italian method, with a different set of exercises for each day of the week. I always wear a light overskirt, tights and ballet shoes, which I sew myself with special thread.

After the lesson I quickly swallow a roll and run off to my rehearsal at the theatrical school. My maid gives me a little packet of sandwiches before I leave, and once at the school I drink tea and eat the sandwiches with great relish, for by now I am starving. The rehearsal, unlike the lesson, is with other members of the ballet company. I work until I am totally exhausted, and when I have a little time between rehearsals I chat with the other dancers or wash my stays.

You know, we observe a very strict etiquette both on the stage and at rehearsals. Younger dancers must obey the orders of their seniors and address them as 'vy', that is, the more formal 'you'. But the older dancers call the younger ones the more familiar 'ty'. For example, I call Kchessinskaya 'vy, Malya' and she calls me 'ty, Annuchka'. The same applies to Preobrajenskaya and the others, the only exception being Pavel Gerdt, who taught us all at school and whom we all love.

When the rehearsal is over I run home to eat, for by then I am tired, irritable and hungry. You probably think that a ballerina exists on little candies and airy little pies. Not at all! We all love very heavy and very simple Russian cooking. My own particular favourites are herring and *Kasha* [Russian porridge], black bread and butter, and pressed gingerbread. I have no wish to depict us an unearthly creatures. Of course, if you invite a ballerina to dinner in a restaurant and ask her what she would like, she will probably order grouse and caviare, because these are considered delicacies. On the day of a performance

Caricature of Pavlova with the eminent ballet critic Valerian Svetlov.

most ballerinas cannot eat a thing. Not I! At five o'clock I have a cup of bouillon, a cutlet and a custard dessert. During the performance I drink water with breadcrumbs, which is most refreshing. After the ballet I have a bath as soon as possible. Then I go out to dinner, as by that time I have an unmerciful hunger. When I get home I drink tea.

The next morning I seize the newspapers and quickly read the reviews. My first impression produces either happy smiles or grim despair. Then I read them again more carefully and decide if what has been written is true or biased, keeping in mind any criticism that seems justified.

Almost every evening I am busy at ballet and opera rehearsals and performances, so I very rarely have any free time to go to the theatre or visit friends. There is an old saying that those who want to develop their legs must forget about their head. I must confess that during the ballet season I read very little, as I have so little time and when I get home I am so tired that I fall asleep with a book on my lap.

How little the daily life of a ballet dancer in a large, permanent company has changed since Pavlova's youth! The dancers have no worries about their costumes or hairdressing, which are seen to by the wardrobe department and the hairdressers; shoes are given out by the shoe department and rehearsals are scheduled by ballet-masters to take place in the company studios, where pianists await with music ready.

All the dancer has to do is to prepare her ballet shoes (in Pavlova's time they sewed a thick layer of stitching on the toe to preserve the satin and soften the sound of blocked toe on the stage – we did the same when I was young: a noisy shoe was a sin), and 'wash her stays' or whatever is current rehearsal wear. Dancers do a lot of laundry.

Apart from that the dancer must dance *and that is the single focus of energy every day. The morning class is essential to keep in training and prepare for rehearsal and performance. The rehearsal can be long and exhausting, while the performance consumes an extraordinary amount of physical and nervous energy. Such work cannot be done on an empty stomach!*

'Madame has introduced into Russia the Beresford breed of bulldogs.'

Below The small touring troupe on the eve of their departure. Pavlova is seated third on the left.

Left Programme for *La Fille Mal Gardée*, Riga, 28 February 1908.

After I had been ballerina for three years I made my first tour.... No one outside of Russia knew anything of Russian dancing ... with the exception of those who occasionally visited Moscow or St Petersburg. When our tour was first suggested, it met a terrible thundering of disapproval. But the clamour was stilled by some secret and adroit diplomacy and permission was given for us to undertake the pilgrimage.

The St Petersburg dancers occasionally made individual guest appearances abroad, for which they had to have the consent of the Tsar, who traditionally supported the Imperial theatres out of his personal budget. This permission was usually granted without hindrance through the theatre directorate.

It was most unusual, however, for a whole group from the Maryinsky ballet to go off on a tour taking with them the company productions with scenery and costumes. Nevertheless, this was how Pavlova, who had by now a strong following among the powerful balletomanes, began her 'world wanderings' – in the course of which she learned of many strange things in foreign lands.

Until I left Russia on the first of my tours, I never dreamed that in the public mind the life of an artist is usually put down as synonymous with a life of personal degradation. It seemed unbelievable to me, like some ghastly joke, that when people encountered in my travels spoke of a girl becoming a dancer, they used the same tone they would have whispered of her entrance into the oldest profession in the world.

At the Imperial Conservatory we were as guarded, as cherished, as protected, as any child trained in a convent. And amazing as it may seem, when the gay, colourful, ecstatic nature of our profession is considered, there was a severity, a simplicity about our daily thought and living that was almost Quakerish. ... We grew up with the conviction that art was very close to God and therefore very sacred; and for us to commit any act that would degrade or defile that art would have been as much profanation to us as to have gone marauding in a sanctuary.⋆

People imagine we lead a frivolous life; the fact is we cannot. We have to choose between frivolity and our art. The two are incompatible.

Pavlova danced in Riga in 1908 and was an instant success. It is not hard to see in group photographs how she stood out from her more robust colleagues. Many people would have labelled her as 'painfully thin' (an expression I remember from my youth – though it was never applied to me!). However, she had by now succeeded in developing the stamina and hidden strength that she required, and above all she poured a wealth of emotion into her performances.

This period began her golden years, the glorious spring and summer of Pavlova's career when everything was exciting and fresh, successes fell into her lap like ripe cherries, and her hopes were realized one after another.

Following Riga, she couldn't wait to set out for other cities and other countries.

Pavlova in *La Fille Mal Gardée*.

I ventured into Scandinavia, and for the first time enjoyed the thrill of being welcomed by royalty. I looked on this as one more milestone passed on the hard road to fame; but even then I realized that where I must rule was in the hearts of the people.

Still unused to renown, I could not quite understand why numbers of people began to gather outside my hotel window after the theatre each night and refused to depart until I spoke to them from the balcony. Once I remarked on it to my maid, a simple Russian peasant girl. She replied, 'Madame, one can easily appreciate their feelings. You make them forget for an hour their sad, hard lives, their sorrows, their poverty. They come to thank you.'

I have earned few tributes which I value higher than that.

Pavlova's words 'where I must rule was in the hearts of the people' stand out so strongly as I read that passage that I see them as the very centre of her driving force in later years when she was increasingly obsessed with transmitting the beauty of art to everyone in the wide world. At the same time, like most of us, she was certainly not immune to the excitement of meeting royalty and receiving their compliments.

The first monarch I met outside my own country was the late King Oscar of Sweden. When I was at Stockholm he came every evening to see the ballet. He knew all the dancers and was familiar with their specialities. Now and then he made comments, which were perfectly just. One had to 'take care of one's p's and q's' in the presence of such a critic!

One evening the King invited me, quite unceremoniously, for the next day. I was not then acquainted with State ceremony. I only knew that I was to be ready at a certain hour. Long before the appointed time I was waiting in the hall of my hotel. A gala carriage, which might well have dated from the eighteenth century, came to the door, one of the King's aides-de-camp offered me his arm, the crowd looked on, and I drove off to the palace like a princess!

At first I was led into a hall, which, like all tourists who visit the royal palace, I already knew. It had never occurred to me that anyone could *live* in these places. Suddenly the King stood before me, and immediately began to talk about dancing. This gave me confidence. . . .

The King asked me if I could not introduce a Spanish dance in my evening programme to please him. It was not easy to procure a suitable costume at such short notice, but I appeared that evening as a Spanish dancer, and received a decoration, which his Majesty brought himself; there was no formality about it. . . .

The decoration made me feel very proud. It is, after all, a beautiful feeling to be rewarded for something which comes quite naturally to us, and to which we are so devoted that we could not refrain from it, even if heavy penalties awaited us. It is a fine thing to receive a decoration just for dancing!

Such a happy sentiment! One can just picture Pavlova, still a little surprised by her success, and a little awed, perhaps, to find herself treated already like a great international star, even received by the King of Sweden, and given a decoration – a reward for doing just the thing she couldn't give up if she tried! I love that!

The following year was 1909. Serge Diaghilev, who was so much more than just an impresario, presented a sensational first season of Russian ballet in Paris. He wanted Pavlova, but her prior engagements in Germany and Austria prevented her from dancing at the opening performances. They turned into a triumph for Karsavina and Nijinsky.

It goes without saying that Pavlova overwhelmed the Paris audiences when she, too, joined the season but she was never, at heart, an artist who could fit into the innovative and intellectual atmosphere that Diaghilev created around him, and of which he was absolute master. Pavlova conquered alone.

Opposite Pavlova with Nicolas Legat in *Swan Lake*, Berlin, 1909.

Above In the Chopin *valse*.

Opposite 'I appeared in flowing, greyish-blue garments, holding white lilies.'

While Pavlova was dancing in Paris in 1909 she received an invitation which clearly delighted her. (After all, France was a republic – no King!)

I can remember as though it were yesterday that chance meeting with King Edward, which was the real cause of my coming to England.

It was at the close of a very successful season in Paris that I was invited to dance at a reception given by Lady Londesborough at her London house.*

During the performance the audience was seated so near that I could see everybody's face.

The close proximity of those richly apparelled human beings seemed to rejoice me. . . . I felt I should like to gain the goodwill of each of them. As I took a swift glance around the room it seemed as if everybody was obliged to move with me – as if they all followed my dance while they stood still! I danced for each one and for all!

I did not yet know which among them was the King: but when I saw Queen Alexandra it gave me a shock – so much does she resemble her sister, the Empress Marie. For a moment I thought I was again at St Petersburg, and this thought reassured me, because at first I was afraid of all these people, all strangers to me, who scarcely moved a feature when they spoke to each other, so that I could not tell whether my dancing pleased them or not.*

The programme? Well, I danced first with M. Mordkin to a *valse* and two mazurkas of Chopin. I wore an exact replica of the costume which in the thirties Taglioni, the great Italian ballerina, wore in Paris and London. . . .

The second number was . . . to 'La Nuit' of Rubinstein. In this I appeared in flowing greyish-blue garments, holding white lilies. The King and Queen seemed eagerly to appreciate the charm of that dance, for they applauded with much enthusiasm.

[Then] M. Mordkin and I appeared in Russian dances. Naturally I wore one of our old national garbs – a sarafan of white and gold tissue and . . . a quaint and costly headgear, half tiara and half diadem.★

The King came towards me. But had I not been prepared I should not have known it was his Majesty, for there was nothing to distinguish him from the other gentlemen. . . . He spoke simply and naturally, as people in society speak. He said a few kind words to me in the manner of a well-bred man of the world, not patronizingly, but naturally. But in conversation with a lady one saw that he spoke as the first gentleman of his country.★

The Queen – how young she looked in her beautiful mauve dress! – complimented me and my partner in a most cordial manner.

Just as their Majesties were leaving Cassano's band struck up 'Paraguay', a South American tune, to which I have danced hundreds of times. The Queen turned. 'I know this air so well,' she exclaimed, and I was asked to give this encore.★

I was desolated, for I had to tell her Majesty that I had no costume for the 'Paraguay'.

'Well, dance it as you are,' was the command.★

I did so, and anxious to make a good impression, I exerted myself to the utmost, despite the difficult handicap of my Russian costume. I shall never forget that warm experience! At the end I was almost fainting with fatigue, for it was a midsummer day. But in the knowledge that I had danced my best, I was more than content.

How curious the whole scene appears to us now! If Pavlova were to dance before the Royal Family in London today it would, of course, be on the stage of the Royal Opera House and she would be received afterwards in the salon behind the Royal Box.

But she is talking of 1909 when there was no Royal Opera Company and still less a Royal Ballet. For someone brought up in a theatre supported personally by the Tsar it was extraordinary how Pavlova and other great ballerinas accepted the dismal lack of suitable theatres in London, where ballet could be seen only in music halls.

Pavlova in her heavy Russian costume.

This St Petersburg portrait calls to mind the words of one New York critic who, in 1910, wrote of 'the inscrutable, wistful, questioning expression of the deep-set eyes'.

Before she returned to St Petersburg, Pavlova happily signed a contract to dance at London's Palace Theatre the following spring.

Although she was dazzled by her conquests in Germany and Paris, she still regarded herself as very much a ballerina of the Maryinsky Theatre. Yet one can tell that she felt constrained by the limited repertoire available to her in Russia. Among her reasons for taking frequent leave of absence was her hunger for new roles – curiously it is the same reason that now brings us the so-called defectors from Russia. In a way, Pavlova was the original defector.

Two interviews she gave in St Petersburg in 1909 reveal her ambivalence at that moment. There is still a touch of naïveté in her outlook, and although at twenty-eight she has a high degree of success and fame, she is not yet the 'Incomparable'.

My trips abroad have had a great effect on me. I was moved by the successes bestowed upon me in Sweden, Denmark and Germany. The Germans, in particular, understand and value me. Perhaps it's because before them I performed the dances which are liked at home. They love pure art. . . .

In Paris, Russian art was served up like Russian food, too luxuriously and too copiously. Individual performers were lost, and I didn't even perform there the dances in which I had made my name here and in Germany. I asked Diaghilev to put on *Giselle* without any frills, without elaborate scenery, but he was afraid. . . .

What am I to do if there aren't any new productions here as there used to be? Don't you think I would be happy if they were to create and produce a ballet specially for Pavlova?★

Q. Is it true that you intend to leave Russia for ever?

Actually, I was offered an engagement in New York for a whole year, but I agreed to go for only two months – February and March. I've been invited to the famous Metropolitan Opera House, and I'm to be paid 40,000 francs a month, with first-class travel there and back. Aren't these splendid conditions? I shall dance *Coppélia* in New York and a divertissement of my own choice. . . . Following this I shall dance at the Palace Theatre in London. So I shall be abroad all of the coming spring and summer.

I have no wish to break completely with Russia.

The memory of my childhood, my first steps on the stage and my first success is associated with St Petersburg. I would never leave Russia for ever. . . . Anyway the [Maryinsky] management has offered me the highest salary a ballerina has ever received. I have signed a contract for a salary of 6,000 roubles for the first year, 7,000 for the second, and 8,000 for the third. Only Vazem and Sokolova have ever received this sort of money, and then only when they were at the height of their fame.

You must remember that at the end of my career I shall receive a pension in Russia. That's something I won't get abroad. Furthermore, the management offered me these conditions because they feared I might be 'abducted'. And they are well aware that there are not so many ballerinas about at the present time.

Q. So because there are so few ballerinas you really will have considerably more work?

Certainly! But I'm not afraid of work.

Q. What are you going to dance this season?

At present I am rehearsing *Sleeping Beauty*, but I don't know what I shall be given after that. The management always keeps its plans to itself.

Q. You said you were going to dance in London at the Palace Theatre. Don't you agree with Diaghilev that it is unworthy of artists of the Imperial Theatres to appear in these *cafés-chantant*?

I entirely disagree with Diaghilev. Only if you know nothing about London and the English could you possibly call this theatre a *café-chantant*. For a start, nothing is eaten or drunk there, and the audience is most refined. The ladies are all in ball-dress and the gentlemen wear frock-coats. Furthermore, the theatre has a Royal Box. You know as well as I that the King of England would never go to a *café-chantant*. There are no *chansonettes* . . . nor any signs of nudity – nor, indeed, any obscenities. There are several such 'variety' theatres in London . . . the Palace is considered the classiest. . . .

Anyway, there are simply no other theatres for ballerinas to dance in abroad. . . . Choreographic art has declined terribly everywhere, in Paris, Berlin, Milan. . . . It's not much use dancing in such poor surroundings – but one must dance somewhere.

Reading between the lines of that last interview, I feel that the writer had set out to provoke her in any way he could, and she defended herself with a few jibes at the directorate of the Imperial Theatre, and at Diaghilev as well, for good measure. Defensively, too, she talked of her contracts; she is still young and a little insecure in her position.

It isn't hard to understand that the stay-at-home critics and balletomanes of St Petersburg were dismayed to find all their favourites suddenly rushing abroad at any opportunity. They themselves had been so sure that they were in the very centre of the ballet world and they didn't like to see all this fuss in Paris, Berlin, London. Now Pavlova was talking of New York — and for a whole year! No wonder they were upset with her.

In fact her first visit to America lasted only six weeks, and she appeared with the Metropolitan Opera. It was in the spring of 1910. Here is a description of her shortly after her arrival.

Mlle Pavlova — or Pavlow, Pavlouva, Pavlov, take your choice — comes to this country with the heartiest endorsement of Paris, where they know good dancing when they see it. When you meet her you do not need to know beforehand that she is a dancer, however, for the multitudinous serpentine motions and sinuous gestures with which she emphasizes her conversation would quickly apprise any one of the fact. Seated in her charming apartments at the Hotel Knickerbocker on the day after her arrival in America, she confided to a representative of *Musical America* with an alacrity that was most startling that she was over twenty-one years of age — yes, and more than that, that she was twenty-seven. She said it without hesitation, without having been asked, and with two lithe, upward flourishes of her graceful arms. On being told that she did not look it, she replied that she did.

'Yes, I am twenty-seven,' she repeated thoughtfully, in a slightly Russianized French that was charming, 'and I have been on the stage for ten years, dancing, always dancing. . . .

'I had to study and practice for eight years before even starting, and to this day I have to keep at it like an athlete in training. There are a thousand and one things you must keep thinking of in dancing. The slightest motion, the least gesture must have its purpose and its meaning. You must manage your breath with more care than a singer. You must be paying attention to the position of your toes, to the motion of your arms, to the expression on your face. And all that is only a little of it. There are rehearsals and rehearsals and still more rehearsals. And when there are no more rehearsals, there are the performances. Yes, it means work, and a good deal of it.'

The first part of that interview is even more charming when one knows that actually she was twenty-nine. But it was accepted custom for every woman to put the clock back a little, and what better opportunity to do so — and to make it very definite — than on her arrival in a country, or rather on a continent, that scarcely even knew her name.

What I find extremely interesting is Pavlova's concise analysis of a dancer in performance and how she must think of a thousand things at once. I personally always found it very difficult to explain, and rarely would an interviewer grasp so accurately what was said.

As she continued the interview, Pavlova was clearly anxious to make known that she would have preferred to be seen in one of the ballets — like Giselle — *of the serious, classical repertoire in which she excelled. Although she was apparently enchanting in* Coppélia, *the principal role is for a soubrette. The incredible thing was that the programme opened with the opera* Werther — *all four acts! And the ballet followed at around 11.00 p.m.*

There we are set down for *Coppélia* at our first appearance. *Coppélia* — a thing that everybody has seen a thousand times! Of course, when you have to crowd it into forty short minutes after an opera you can't be expected to do very much. Why, look! In Europe there are ballets given that occupy an entire evening — ballets in four or five acts, just like a play or opera. In Russia we have special theaters built for them. You haven't acquired a taste for these yet, have you? . . .

Come to the Metropolitan . . . and I hope you will enjoy yourself. You can judge better with scenery and costumes than you can from any further descriptions I could give you. Just now I am dreadfully upset. None of my trunks have come from the custom house as yet. *C'est embêtant!* An awful nuisance!

Opposite As Swanilda in *Coppélia*. 'Grace, a certain sensuous charm, and a decided sense of humor.'

New York

Very annoying to have one's trunks delayed in customs, but at least she knew they had arrived with her. In these days of air travel, one is always nervous that one's costumes and ballet shoes might have gone to Alaska by mistake. On the other hand, it is terribly difficult to keep in training on a voyage by ship and, in addition, Pavlova suffered badly from sea-sickness. That is probably why she talks of feeling better in an interview for the New York Times *entitled 'A Great Dancer Discusses Her Life and Art'.*

Anna Pavlova, the Russian dancer who has created such a genuine sensation in New York, a slim, dark-eyed, dark-haired young woman, was seated in a rocking chair in her room at the Knickerbocker Hotel, eating candy, resting after her matinée performance, and talking as rapidly as she can dance.

'I feel much better now than on the day of my arrival in New York,' she remarked.

'Do you think that your success in New York has something to do with the improvement in your health?'

'Oh, no, this success cannot affect me,' she smiled. 'We have been spoiled by success everywhere, in Russia, in Germany, in France, and in England. But I feel happy, nevertheless, that our art is appreciated in this country. You see, in Europe we make a specialty of the ballet, while here I understand it is merely incidental. In Russia particularly, the ballet is a branch of art to which much attention is paid and dancing is one of the favorite amusements of the Tsar.'

'Have you ever seen the Tsar?'

'Have I ever seen the Tsar?' repeated Mlle Pavlova, her dark eyes half smiling, half surprised. 'Why, he stroked my hair when I was a pupil – he praised me. He used to come to our school and talk to us and tell jokes and eat dinner with us – the same things we used to eat.'

'Did the Tsar tell clever jokes?'

'I can't remember any of them now,' replied the little dancer. . . .

'In Russia my day is crowded with work. . . . I rehearse until four o'clock. . . . Then I go home. I glance over the newspapers and read a few pages of my favorite poet or my favorite novelist. . . .

'From five to six in the afternoon I receive. There are many artists, painters, sculptors among my friends. But I devote only one hour to them. In the evening I sometimes have additional rehearsals. When I do not perform and have no rehearsals in the evening, I go to the theatre. I prefer the drama – the heart-stirring drama. Occasionally I go to a good concert. When some celebrated artist visits St Petersburg, such as Nikisch, for instance, I always go to hear him, and that is a real holiday for me. I love music and I enjoy animals. I have a fine English bulldog at home. Well, what else can I say? That is all, that is my life.'

'Are you interested in any of the sports?'

'I need no sports of any kind. Occasionally I go horseback riding, but that isn't very good for me. I must keep my body in a certain position for a long time when I am on horseback, and this interferes with my art. You see, I do not need any of the sports because my art combines them all. . . . My work, my art is developing every muscle of my body. . . . There is but one thing I love passionately, outside of my art, and that is nature. The cold, dreamy forests appeal to me, to my imagination. Tropical plants do not interest me so much. You cannot dream under palm trees. . . .'

Mlle Pavlova helped herself to some more candy and . . . began to speak of New York.

'I haven't seen anything here as yet. I haven't had time. You know, life here seems to be rushing at a maddening pace. It is like a crazy wheel, revolving with lightning-like rapidity. I am afraid that it would be hard to keep pace with it. By the way, a young woman asked me about marriage. She wanted to know whether it was true that I haven't married because I have not had the time. . . . In America that must seem strange, for here I understand – one, two, three,' she snapped her fingers, 'and you are married. There is no time to waste. And then – one, two, three – and you're divorced. In Russia such an event in a person's life is considered slowly and carefully; the couple must . . . first find out whether their characters are suited for each other; they reflect; they deliberate; they go through the poetic period of wooing; and then they marry. . . . Such a step is indeed an event, and it really takes up much time. Besides, I believe that artists who are really devoted to their art should not think of marriage.'

Opposite Pavlova in 1910.

For her first visit to America Pavlova had chosen Mikhail Mordkin as her partner, although he was not from the St Petersburg school but from Moscow. Described as a 'wonderful specimen of manhood', he was dark, handsome and an astounding dancer and artist on the stage, providing the perfect foil to Pavlova's femininity. Together they made a triumph in New York and the eastern states of America, then set sail across the Atlantic – this time to challenge, and conquer, the British.

She gives the impression that she was more nervous than on any occasion before. She had explained to the critic in St Petersburg a few months earlier that the Palace Theatre, although a variety house, had a Royal Box and the audiences were most refined. Nevertheless, the Russian dancers shared the programme with 'such clever entertainers as Horace Goldin, the extraordinary illusionist, and Mr Albert Whelan, the amusing Australian comedian'. The critic for the Tatler, *27 April 1910, found the other numbers 'a trifle mediocre and rather dull. Even the ever-welcome Palace girls could not wake things up.' Then he described the atmosphere in the house as the programme progressed.*

As the turn of the evening approached ... that mysterious sense of electricity which should always permeate between the entertainers and the entertained began to assert itself. The house was packed from floor to ceiling with that well-dressed audience which hardly any other music hall in London besides the Palace can ever manage to show. Would the celebrated Pavlova meet with the same triumph in London as had been accorded her already in Berlin, Paris, and New York?

Pavlova was never to forget that London debut.

So I stood on the stage before my first English audience, trembling with excitement.... They seemed not to care....

I began to fear failure....

At last I stopped and there was a moment of silence, during which the whole world seemed to stand still. Then, suddenly, the whole theatre was clapping, shouting, as though electricity had galvanized a painted theatre all to life.

I cried, I laughed, I held out my hands to them, for I knew I had conquered! I think it is well for us mortals that there are not many such moments in our lives, for at such times we become the equals of the gods themselves.

Pavlova and Mordkin in *Valse Caprice*. 'To see her in his arms throwing back her head in an attitude of would-be escape brings the house to that point of murmured admiration which is very rarely heard in England.'

II

I have always secretly dreamed of spending the second half of my career abroad, and it has turned out that way. . . . I have signed a contract in America and must leave St Petersburg on 3 September, so perhaps I shall have time to appear once before the public to say goodbye.

Of course, these two years will pass very quickly, like everything in life. Naturally I will be criticized for leaving the Maryinsky stage, but that is wrong. I personally am proud of my engagement – and I will get a huge fee.

I worked honestly in St Petersburg for ten years, and I shall leave behind the memory of myself as a good artiste and give the young dancers an opportunity to perform all the best roles. At the same time I will show Russian art abroad; and, after two or three years, while I am still young, I will have some capital and worldwide renown as a dancer.

This is Pavlova at almost thirty. The year is 1910. No longer the naïve venturer, she has made her name in the capitals of Europe and tasted success in New York. Whereas the Maryinsky Theatre was once the centre of her universe, she now casually hopes she will have time to say goodbye to her faithful public there before she leaves to cover the American continent from end to end – and make her fortune.

Messrs. Max Rabinoff and G. P. Centanini

have the honor of announcing the first
American tour of

The Imperial Russian Ballet and Orchestra

(THEODORE STIER, Conductor)

Supporting the Incomparable

Mlle. Anna Pavlowa

Prima Ballerina Assoluta, Imperial Opera House, St. Petersburg

and

M. Mikail Mordkin

Premier Danseur Classique, Imperial Opera House, Moscow

with a distinguished company of character dancers, by special arrangement with the Imperial Russian Government, and the Metropolitan Opera Company, New York, introducing an art new to America, the interpretation of the ponderous messages of the great composers through the most primitive and yet potent of mediums—motion!

PUBLISHED BY

COMSTOCK & GEST (Inc.)

1416 Broadway, New York

MORRIS GEST   Copyright, 1910   F. RAY COMSTOCK

Price, Fifteen Cents

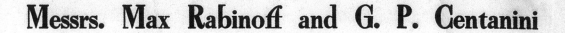

Cover of the souvenir programme for the North American tour, 1910–11.

Above Pavlova as Aziade.

The American impresarios who had contracted Pavlova and Mordkin for a six-month nation-wide tour must have felt themselves caught in a certain predicament. The two Russian dancers were a sensation and, once seen, would inevitably win over the public; of that they were sure. But how could the public be attracted into the theatres in the first place if it had no conception of the entertainment in store?

In their nervousness, and not wanting to advertise the word 'ballet', which evidently terrified them, Messrs Rabinoff and Centanini resorted to the most extraordinary phrases which, one would imagine, risked alienating the public far more.

The programme cover, for example, carried the description 'an art new to America, the interpretation of the ponderous messages of the great composers . . .' and another attempt to anticipate and forestall possible complaints explained, 'Not a line is spoken, not a word sung' during 'the unfolding or enactment of a narrative . . . drama, opera or call it what you may . . . through Terpsichore.'

One can't help thinking that it would have been simpler just to call it ballet.

For this tour Pavlova and Mordkin took Legend of Aziade, a ballet in the Oriental style that was then very much in fashion, and Giselle – which the New York critics rated as old-fashioned with dull music.

Below Posing with Mordkin and company in costume for Legend of Aziade.

Interview in Indiana

Once the company was out on the road Pavlova began to know the real rough and tumble of touring, with its endless repetition of new city – looking very much like the last one – and new stage, with never time to get accustomed to it before moving on. They travelled everywhere by train, often living on it for weeks.

In Indiana, in the mid-west, Ben Atwell, their press agent, arranged for Frank Odell of the Indianapolis Sun *to interview Pavlova at the end of the performance.*

At the door of the star's dressing room I hesitated, asking 'Is she going to be difficult, Ben?'

'Difficult? Anna Pavlova? She likes people. You'll hit it off.' He rapped upon the door and pushed me in ahead of himself.

Pavlova had dropped a frilly ballet skirt, which lay in a circle about her feet. She was attired in a skimpy foundation garment until her costumer tossed a scarf over her shoulders. There was no palaver about immodesty. She was an artist interrupted in her professional routine. I was a reporter pursuing news. When presented to her I bowed, but she extended her slender fingers for a cordial handclasp.

'Ben Atwell said you are city editor. You are too young.'

'*Acting* city editor. That way I do the work, but it costs the paper less money. Tonight I am back to reporting.'

'All the English journalists were much older. How old are you?'

'Twenty-four in July. Do you think the *Sun* sent a boy to do a man's job?'

'I'm sure you will do. Sit here at the end of the dressing table facing me. Have a cigarette?'

'Thank you.' I accepted one of the extra long Russian cigarettes made of perfumed Turkish tobacco.

She drew upon her own, and applied the glowing end to light mine, as I leaned forward slightly. 'Now tell me how good a musician are you? Do you know all about ballet?'

'I know practically nothing about music or ballet, except to enjoy both.'

'Then how can you possibly write about either?'

'Do I have to be a criminal to write of robbery or murder? I am a reporter of five years experience. A journalist learns to observe essentials, and to respond sensitively to nuances of feeling and comprehension. Too many technicalities confuse a reader. Overall impressions go better. When I do not understand clearly enough to pass on information to our readers then I consult someone who does know – like you. Such an authority may be a valuable pipe-line for news.'

'*Pipe-line*? How charming. Can Pavlova be such a thing – a pipe-line to carry information through you to your readers?'

'One of the very best.'

'That I like. Now, what do you   and your readers – want to know?'

'You are the epitome of grace and perfect precision. You will be remembered among the top artists of all times. People who watch you with fascination on the stage ask what started you to dancing, what took you to the top, what does the real Pavlova think and feel?'

'I can explain my professional success in a few words: Pavlova had the strength to work hard and the zeal to put in thousands and thousands of hours striving for perfection. . . .

'Even today I practised this morning four hours, besides doing more work in tonight's performance than most women do in a week. It must be so until the end of my career. . . .'

Michel Mordkin, her *premier danseur*, barged into the room. Pavlova introduced me to him. He nodded casually but did not shake hands. He grunted, paced back and forth, glaring at me, then abruptly stalked out again. Atwell explained: 'He speaks only Russian and French.'

'Is this what you want for your paper?' she asked. 'Is Pavlova a good – what you call – *pipe-line*?'

'Superb. . . . After you complete this tour you will return to Russia to stay?'

'I shall go back. My mother and grandmother are there. But I have seen freedom in the outside world. I shall not spend as much time there as before.'

Giselle. 'Only the pantomime and dancing of Pavlova raised it above the obvious,' reported the *New York World* in 1910.

Interview in Indiana

Frank Odell observed Pavlova closely while he was interviewing her.

Her height was slightly below average. She said that her weight never rose above 108 pounds, although she consumed gallons of cod liver oil in an effort to fatten a little. Her hair was thick and black. Her eyes were dark, set wide below a high forehead. The nose was large, the mouth too wide to be pretty, the cheek bones high and prominent. ... Her complexion was smooth, the skin dead white. ... The arms were adequately muscled and tapered attractively to delicate, small-boned wrists and hands. ... The waist was small. Her uncorsetted figure ... seemed almost boyish in litheness and spare muscularity.

Aesthetic appearances were always important to Pavlova, especially in relation to dancers. She once said:

It is possible to go through the exercises of dancing regularly without in any way over-developing any muscles – at least that is my experience, though I am afraid in many cases dancers do over-develop their muscles, and to some extent make them quite unshapely.

Odell commented on her 'perfect muscular coordination', using an epithet, 'muscle-minded', that delighted her.

Pavlova repeated the word to get its savor. 'Yes, that is it, *muscle-minded*'. ...

'Is it a secret how you achieve such airy, apparently effortless, ease and dignity?'

'Dignity of elevation you get out of the erect line of the back, neck and head. See. Hold the head high. That commands respect. Now for airiness the entire body must be tough, alert and springy. You cushion the blow of descent upon the arch of the foot. That softens the contact with the hard stage as you come down from a high leap. Then the pick-up must be quick as lightning to look buoyant and elastic. ... Of course you must have contempt for weariness and pain. To float so lightly about the stage is the hardest of labor.'

Yes indeed! And Pavlova's marvellously arched insteps, so beautiful to look at, presented certain technical difficulties. Just before the interview Atwell had explained to Odell:

She says herself her feet are not right for a ballet dancer. Her toes are too long, the instep too high. These are great handicaps, overcome only by long practice. ... All her shoes are made by a Milan specialist to fit her plaster casts, tracings and diagrams. ... Her shoe bill is enormous. A man could live well on what her shoes cost every year.

Opposite A rare unpublished portrait.

Below Pavlova at her dressing-table, 1911.

Ballet shoes, or toe shoes, are the bane of every ballerina's life. Some are a dream to wear and others are just wrong from the start. With a few days between one performance and the next, one has a chance to 'break in' several pairs and select the good ones, but this becomes almost impossible when one is dancing every night.

Victor Dandré, who managed Pavlova's company and travelled the world with her, wrote a book on her after her death. Here is what he says about Romeo Nicolini of Milan, who made all her shoes.

On our very first visit to Italy we decided to call on Nicolini in order to discuss certain matters personally with him. With his spectacles pushed back on his forehead while talking, he only answered with one word 'si, si', to everything we said. As he spoke only Italian and our knowledge of that language was limited, his son, who knew a little French, was called to act as interpreter. But Pavlova's patience gave out and, putting on a pair of shoes, she explained what she required, demonstrating the defects of the shoes by performing various *pas*.

In order to ... make him careful in fulfilling his contract, we decided to guarantee him an annual order for a gross of shoes and to pay him rather more than the usual price.

All this was duly written down on paper and we took our departure, Pavlova saying happily to me that Romeo had at last understood everything. But this was rash and premature. We went at least ten times to his shop after that, and each time Pavlova explained everything ... but all to no avail. Invariably each delivery was not so good as the preceding one. ...

We were in Milan again the following year and there met the well-known dancer, Rosina Galli [who] also had her shoes from Romeo. ... We decided to take advantage of the opportunity to go together to Nicolini. I think it was a long time before the old man forgot that visit. Both the dancers put on shoes and began to explain what they required. ... Some days later the shoes arrived and to their horror the dancers found that Nicolini had completely muddled everything, doing for Rosina Galli what was required for Pavlova, and for Pavlova what Rosina Galli had asked for.

In addition to his lack of attention ... Nicolini was very unpunctual. We would give him an order six months in advance, telling him exactly the dates, quantities and places of delivery. ... The first lot of shoes would arrive in time, the second lot would be a month or two late and the third lot would not arrive at all. ... There were more orders than could be executed, and Romeo knew that a dancer, having once got used to his shoes, would never leave him. ... The very natural question arises: why could not Pavlova in all these years find another shoemaker? ... Countless attempts were made, but without success. ...

An American shoemaker in Los Angeles brought her a new pair every day, altering them each time to her instructions and finally produced a pair in which she was able to dance once, but even they were not comfortable. It was Pavlova's opinion that this was because they were made by machinery; as she said 'they had no soul' ....

But from the moment when Maestro Cecchetti went to live in Milan, our task became somewhat simplified. We wrote or telegraphed to him, and either he himself or his wife ... did all in their power to help. ... The Maestro told us later that he once reproached Nicolini for the trouble he was causing a celebrated ballerina.

'Don't you understand what an honour it is for you that the great Pavlova has her shoes made by you?' he asked.

The old man thought a while and then answered:

'Yes, it's a great honour that she is my client.' And reflecting further he added:

'Yes, but if I had two Pavlovas, I'd be done for.'

The funny thing about that story, every bit of which must be without exaggeration exactly as it happened, is that for my first three or four years on the stage I wore only Nicolini shoes. After the old man died, although I found another excellent maker, I always dreamed of the absolute perfection of Nicolini's shoes, compared to which all others seemed to lack some secret magic.

I suspect that, when one blames the shoes, one sometimes forgets that the climate, the stage surface and even one's feet tend to vary from day to day. But we do all know the despair of going through the available shoes and finding barely two that are 'right'. It is one of the causes of tension which is often described as 'temperament'.

'I wonder where all my shoes go? One or two pairs I have kept – the lucky ones.'

Photograph   *Ellis and Walery*
Mlle. Pavlova, who Dances with M. Mordkin

SOME ATTITUDES
OF THE RUSSIAN DANCER
WHO RESENTS
BEING REPRESENTED AS
DANCING SECOND STEP
TO HIS FAIR—
BUT NON-FRIENDLY—
COLLEAGUE,
MLLE. PAVLOVA

'Out of sheer human sympathy for M. Mordkin, who has to subsist on a wretched £175 a week minimum, and doesn't get all the limelight he deserves, we publish these portraits glorifying him for once in a way at the expense of Mlle Pavlova, whom we inset intentionally small.'
A page from *The Bystander*, London, 5 July 1911.

Pavlova, Mordkin and the company finished their long North American tour in April 1911, and, with hardly time to catch their breath, were again appearing at the Palace Theatre, London, for a run of three months.

Stage temperament has always fascinated the press and public alike, and during these legendary performances at the Palace they were treated to an unusually prolonged bout, which ruined the pas de deux, *but gave an obvious piquancy to the season.*

The critic for the Tatler *has left us this tongue-in-cheek account.*

First of all Mordkin bounded upon the stage smiling as if he were suddenly going to bite. . . . There is a sound as of rushing water or a tyre punctured – though the former sounds more poetical – as all the ladies lean forward in their seats to gaze, under the patronage of art, upon a young man built with the powerful proportions of an antique statue, and not at all ashamed of the fact. . . . And how wonderfully Mordkin dances. The precision of his steps is marvellous. All the same I shouldn't like to be standing in the wings at the Palace Theatre during his performances of Giraud's *Variations Grecque*. It must be unpleasant to have arrows shot at you unexpectedly from nowhere. . . .

Afterwards there was a sudden hush. Gradually the footlights died away. Over the stage fell the rays of a pale forget-me-not-blue light. The cupids and roses among which these marvellous Russians dance seemed suddenly bathed in shimmering moonlight. The full rushing notes of Rubinstein's 'La Nuit' throbbed through the air, and there before us stood Pavlova – exquisitely fascinating in a pale blue flowing dress. . . . The gentle unobtrusiveness of her entrance seemed more effective than if she had suddenly bounded upon the stage and stood painfully on one toe as is the usual entrance of *première danseuses* when they wish to please. Then she began to dance – and has the present generation of Londoners seen anything more perfect? The attitude, the grace, the exquisite charm – surely these have never been surpassed. Rubinstein's music – its sadness, its passion, its sensuous abandon – was expressed with an art absolutely incomparable.

In *Papillons* Pavlova was the butterfly incarnate. . . . But perhaps the finest thing of the afternoon was her dancing of *La Rose Qui Meurt*. . . . In it she is content to abandon those marvellously executed feats of virtuosity which although wonderful in themselves always mar in my opinion so many of the dances of these extraordinary artists. Chopin's *valse* lost a great deal by being performed as a solo rather than a *pas de deux*; but *La Danse Russe* was full of character and delightful humour. As for Mordkin's interpretation of Tchaikovsky's variations, they were quite extraordinarily vivid and graceful. . . .

The dancing of Anna Pavlova and Michel Mordkin has now the added attraction of a bloodless warfare. Everybody is talking of the quarrel which prevents these two artists dancing together in those pieces which were the sensational joy of the last London season. Of course, too, everybody has a theory as to its cause. Everybody one meets is waxing furious [because] Pavlova and Mordkin refuse to dance together. Evening papers containing an account of bites and scratches sell like hot cakes. Even the Coronation is forgotten.

The discreet, refined, sedate, unemotional audiences who usually flock into the Palace Theatre carry on a warfare of stamps, boos and bravos . . . having apparently decided that whatever the quarrel between these two incomparable dancers – who ought to know better – may be it shall at once come to an end if noise and shouting can reconcile anybody. It is all quite funny and absurd and somewhat impertinent, but booing is wonderfully catching, and one never knows if one will not get a pretty scene of reconciliation for one's money. So we continue to kick up a great shindy until we get turned out and spread the news of the matinée's disaster and failure throughout the whole of England.

Does anyone know the real cause of the quarrel? They say it was simply that he partnered her badly at one of the performances and, in full view of the public, she slapped his face, which, naturally enough his Russian pride could not accept. Thus was a great partnership extinguished for ever. Mordkin's place was taken by another Muscovite, Laurent Novikoff, before the end of the Palace season.

October found Pavlova appearing with the Diaghilev ballet at Covent Garden, in the historic Opera House which was set until recently in the midst of a vegetable market.

Pavlova and Nijinsky in *Le Pavillon d'Armide*. The photographs were taken in St Petersburg in 1907.

I appeared for the first time at Covent Garden. The place, to an artist, is the goal of great ambition; one feels almost reverent at the thought of those many great ones who have there held the very heart of the world of art and made it throb with them.⋆

It has the age and the old traditions I associate with my theatre in St Petersburg. Covent Garden, too, has such a magnificent stage, but there are certain drawbacks to its situation. If I were very rich, I would move the market somewhere else. Like all artists, I am temperamental, and do not notice the time much, and so I am often late, and then all the traffic round the market makes the effort to reach the theatre even worse.

Fashionable London audiences, in full evening dress, picked their way through vegetable baskets to see the wonderful performances of Diaghilev's Ballet Russe. This large company of fine dancers was a luxurious setting for Pavlova, who danced with Nijinsky for the season.

But in a curious way she seems to have felt that it was a luxury she couldn't afford if she was to take her own art in her own way to people the world over.

*London, Paris, Berlin, New York, Monte Carlo, Buenos Aires, Rio de Janeiro saw the magnificent Diagh-*ilev ballet in all its splendour. They also saw Pavlova dancing The Dying Swan *with her own small company, and never forgot the experience – neither did people who saw her in Calcutta, Sioux City, Yokohama, and heaven knows how many other cities great and small that she touched with her magic, regardless of the difficulties and discouragements that she encountered in the process.*

For example, I cannot help being struck by the sadness of this little snippet of information from the Leeds Mercury *of 4 March 1912 – a mere four months after her successes at Covent Garden with the Diaghilev Ballet Russe.*

In addition to twenty-two dances, and a special 'danse-drame' telling a story of neglected love, written for Mdme Pavlova, there will be St John Hankin's new one-act play, *The Constant Love*, violoncello solos by M. Boni, and an elocutionary interlude by Mr Foster.

Surely it would have been far easier, and more glamorous, for her to have been prima ballerina of the Diaghilev ballet in London, Paris, Berlin, Monte Carlo. . . .

Yet glamour was clearly something she carried with her, no matter where she was or what she was wearing.

Above The epitome of glamour, Berlin, 1913.

Opposite Wearing the necklace presented by her St Petersburg fans.

Day dress – ordinary dress – declared Madame, with an expressive shrug of the shoulders, has no interest for her.

Only a woman who, if she is not Parisian born, has all a Parisienne's 'flair' for dress, can afford to make those revolutionary remarks – and Madame, though she is by birth a Russian, is most certainly a French-woman in her innate sense of chic and charm. Her frock of fine navy serge was quietness itself in style and trimming, but its 'line' was unmistakably of the elect. A long 'shawl' rever of burnt orange cloth faced the completing coat worn with this frock, and was the sole note of colour admitted in its scheme. The low-cut, almost décolleté, neck, which is fashion's latest whim, had also been adopted by Madame, and her quaint little moleskin helmet hat, with its great butterfly bow in gold lace, formed the ideal comple-ment to a regal set of moleskins that were also inset with gold lace.

That was written by Our Lady Representative of the Leeds Mercury, *and if Pavlova could impress her, or anyone else, as a woman of supreme elegance while wearing that moleskin helmet with all that gold lace trimming, then she must indeed have been a unique phenomenon on and off the stage – who could doubt it? The article went on to tell the readers that Pavlova spoke in an engagingly impartial mélange of English, French, Russian and Italian, and finished with the words: 'The famous Russian possesses a diamond necklace subscribed for in the smallest coins of the realm by the "Gods" of the St Petersburg theatre.'*

A close friend of Pavlova's took her on a shopping spree shortly before the Leeds appearances. Perhaps she bought the moleskin helmet at Selfridges?

Who could resist the invitation? Anna Pavlova in the theatre is an unapproachable wonder. 'In the life', as she expresses it herself, she is a dear little friend, as little like the typical artist as can be. A little pathetic sometimes and the least ready to assert her own wonderful individuality of any woman I have ever met. But she is so seldom 'in the life' that the chance of going shopping was seized with delight by both of us. We set forth after many alarms and false starts two hours later than we meant to. And how it rained!

Madame Pavlova, a quietly garbed little lady, ran from her motor-car across the wet pavement of Oxford Street, through the wide-open doors of a great shop. . . .

'Where do we begin? But how many people here today!' Her white-gloved hand sought to hide itself in my muff. . . .

'I think,' she said, as she wrapped herself in an ermine stole . . . 'that everything is so *bon marché* in this London and here in this shop so chic. . . .' And the furs went down to the waiting car. . . .

'I have never been shown rubbish in a London shop. . . . I like, too, the idea to let me wander about a shop – such as this house of Selfridge – without worrying me to choose all the time.

'Now, shall we dress ourselves in patelots? . . . Will you ask for me please?' . . . She pretends that English is beyond her and gazes as if deaf and dumb. . . . I move away to examine a cloak. . . . When I come back the hypocrite is talking English . . . and well understanding the attendant's replies. She looks like a child discovered in mischief, and hastily wraps herself in a cloak of soft silk, grey-green in colour, with deep collar and cuffs of grey fox. 'Is it the size for me? . . . I can wear it in the day or night. It is an economy to have such a beautiful coat.' . . . She bought another for travelling as well.

Another shopper passed while we waited for the lift. She had a tiny dog in her arms. 'Oh! that little dog. . . . It reminds me of my dog. Left behind this time in Russia. He is ill, in character, but not wicked. I do not know what to do with him. He is badly brought up. . . .

'What shall we buy next? Hats? . . . But is not this I have on charming? I found it when I came through Paris. Just grey chinchilla and little fluffy white feathers. Now do you think £26 was too much? Someone told me that it was a terrible price. But so pretty and comfortable.'

So she tried on hats . . . flitting from one glass to another . . . moving her head and body to try the effect of some particular *chapeau* in half a dozen dainty poses. Selfridge's millinery department ceased to be a shop; it became a studio, a stage on which moved the most graceful figure in Europe, and the assembled attendants composed an admiring audience, though compelled to silent applause.

'Somebody looks,' whispers the shopper. . . . 'Come away quickly, let us have our tea.' We fled to the Palm Court, Anna Pavlova speeding up the stairs like thistledown in spite of the wet-weather boots. . . .

Over tea she told me . . . that it had been the dream of her life to conquer London. And now, having conquered London, she is going to tour the provinces, to conquer there, too. . . .

'Next summer I want to found a school of dancing in London. I want to train some English children. . . . I will be with them and see their talent grow. . . .

'Oh! my friend, I have a little rehearsal . . . in twenty minutes, and I have many more things to buy. May we come again tomorrow? . . .'

We were to start from the hotel at eleven o'clock. . . . 'The sun is shining. I must wear a new gown. . . .

'I did enjoy yesterday. . . . London shopping is more fascinating every time. How much we did on a rainy day. . . . In Vienna I would not have accomplished nearly so much, for I should have been in six shops instead of only one. In Paris my automobile would have been up and down the Rue de la Paix, to the Louvre, everywhere. . . .

'Everything is good in England, and your shops are best. I have never done so much shopping since I came to London. . . .'

The first department we came to when we again entered Selfridge's was devoted to hosiery. . . . 'Now,' she said, 'I must buy plenty of stockings and gloves. . . . It would astonish you if you knew how many stockings I use in the year. More for "the scene" than for "the life". All these are silk stockings. I wear silk for my dance – I must – but for my life – have you any in cotton, please, like these? . . .

'I will tell you . . . something else I have liked to find here and bought very much of. Silverware. The most beautiful things are made in silver in England, and whenever I wish to send some very nice present to my friends in Russia I send silver. . . .'

Before we finally left the shop of many attractions Madame Pavlova attempted to make a calculation of what she had purchased, used many pieces of paper and finally gave up the idea.

Pavlova 'in the life', 1911.

I soon found after I had been a little while in the country that England was my spiritual home. There only could I find absolute rest, quiet, somewhere I might retreat from the rush and turmoil, somewhere I and my swans could be alone. So it was in England, after much searching and disappointment, that at last I found what I felt to be the ideal place. In all the world, I feel, there cannot be another home of peace and contentment as mine, within a moment's call of one of the world's largest cities.

Ivy House had the immense advantage of a large practice studio and a light semi-basement, where costumes and scenery could be stored. Also a beautiful garden.

A garden? Oh, yes, a very big one, with all sorts of flowers. I dig the flowers, and work with them, make them bloom all summer, and get myself dirty like a pig, yes. [And she laughed and clapped her hands.] I own birds, too, and they sing for me, but I like best the wild birds.∗

The King of Spain sent flowers to Ivy House. He had seen me dancing at the Palace Theatre the day before, and took an interest in the dancing school which I had opened in London. We soon got into conversation, in which the Queen took an eager part, and I so far forgot with whom I was talking as to suggest that their Majesties should postpone the day of their departure from London to witness a performance of my pupils!

Before he left, the King sent me a basket of orchids from a flower shop, with a card, in the same way any other gentleman would have done.

With touching humility Pavlova seemed to imagine that new Pavlovas were everywhere just waiting to be discovered; and she had selected a small group of young girls to teach, herself, at Ivy House.

It is simply wonderful how they have grasped my ideas, dancing absolutely as if they were grown-up artists. I never let the children do anything without making them understand what they are doing and why they are doing it. My idea is not that they should show the technique they possess, but that they should use this technique as a means of expression. No one must see technique: it must be the servant, not the master.

Opposite Three of Pavlova's pupils at Ivy House. In the centre is Muriel Stuart, who was so talented that she later became a member of Pavlova's company.

Below Ivy House, London.

A Ballerina's Home

Undoubtedly Ivy House became Pavlova's only real haven in the long years of exile that were soon to become her fate. Here is a description, from the magazine Home Chat, *of the house as it was in 1924.*

It is at Ivy House, Hampstead, that the incomparable Pavlova has gathered ... those works of art with which, as a great artiste, she loves to surround herself. ...

'I love London best of all,' she said, 'and I look forward to coming back to my London home at the end of my tours. ... She smiled with that charming glow which seems to illuminate her wonderful dark eyes when she smiles. 'Of course I have brought with me marvellous bibelots from my Russian home, which I may, alas, never see more. ... Yes,' she said,

answering my query, 'I like Russian dishes best, and my chef is a Russian; but I like many of your English dishes, too – I like very much the fruit pies of which the English are so fond.'

It was an afternoon in late summer ... and I noticed when I entered the square hall that there seemed to be a faint mimosa-like perfume about everything, but that, I thought, could not be at this time of year in England. Then I was brought into the large conservatory where there was a mimosa tree in full flower. ...

There are few who know that when Pavlova returns, tired out from rehearsing, she 'rests' by sketching or modelling in the delightful room which she calls her work-room or painting-room. This room, by the way, is a symphony in deep mauve and silver. From the window a splendid view can be had on a fine day over the tree tops and far away.

Above A rare moment of relaxation in the garden.
Opposite Pavlova's household on the lawn at Ivy House.

This painting-room leads into Pavlova's bedroom, which opens on to a balcony big enough to form a small lounge. It is a delightful spot to have breakfast on a summer morning. . . .

The furniture in this room has been brought from Russia, the bed, in the Italian style, being carved with garlands of tiny roses and panels of wicker or cane.

Gold, mauve and blue brocade forms the bed-spread, the curtains to the French windows being of lilac mauve silk over lace. The carpet is also in a soft shade of mauve, which seems to be a favourite shade of Pavlova's.

A gallery runs right round the dancing-room, or studio, which is a spacious apartment with a parquet floor, the walls being white-panelled, while blue cushions on the chairs and settees strike a charming note of colour. . . . Here occasionally to the favoured few she dances. It is here also that she teaches those who have the honour to call themselves 'pupils of Pavlova'.

The dining room overlooks the lawn and gardens which, when I saw them, were gay with geraniums.

In a side window stands a fine mahogany inlaid table, and on this there is a priceless crystal set with a large punchbowl in the centre. In this bowl Pavlova herself makes a most delicious punch, for which she alone has the recipe. Fancy those hands which artists have raved about making punch!

One wall in the inner drawing-room is taken up by a cabinet in which are numerous artistic and beautiful souvenirs of the artiste's world tours. . . . It would be impossible to tell of all these treasures, but to each there is attached some reminiscence of the giver.

Most of the furniture in the drawing-room has come from Russia, and is of white carved and inlaid wood. There is, however, a fine Chinese lacquer table and a black velvet chair makes a striking, though sombre, note against the deep cream walls and the old-gold silk curtains. . . . Here, as in all the rooms, there is a profusion of flowers and tall, graceful palms. . . .

All the windows at the back of the house command lovely views of the lawn sloping down to the pond, on which two stately swans move gracefully.

Of my pets the swans are, of course, my favourites because I so love to dance *The Dying Swan*. . . . They are very fond of me, principally because, the gluttons, I feed them cakes and crackers. . . .

When, as will happen now and then, I take my work too seriously and grow introspective and sad . . . I watch the swans; then I call Fifi, the gazelle, and then I don't take myself so seriously. Why? Because I realize that nature is greater than art. My swans and my gazelle are, oh, so graceful without an effort at all, and I must work so hard. I say to myself, 'Oh, to be a swan or a gazelle!' But soon I say, 'No.' For though they are, without giving thought to it, so wonderfully graceful, they are not the intellectual ecstacy and joy that comes from hard work and things accomplished.

Nature is greater than art, but the mind is greater than all things else.

Left and below With Jack, her favourite swan.

Opposite Posing by the lake in *The Dying Swan* costume.

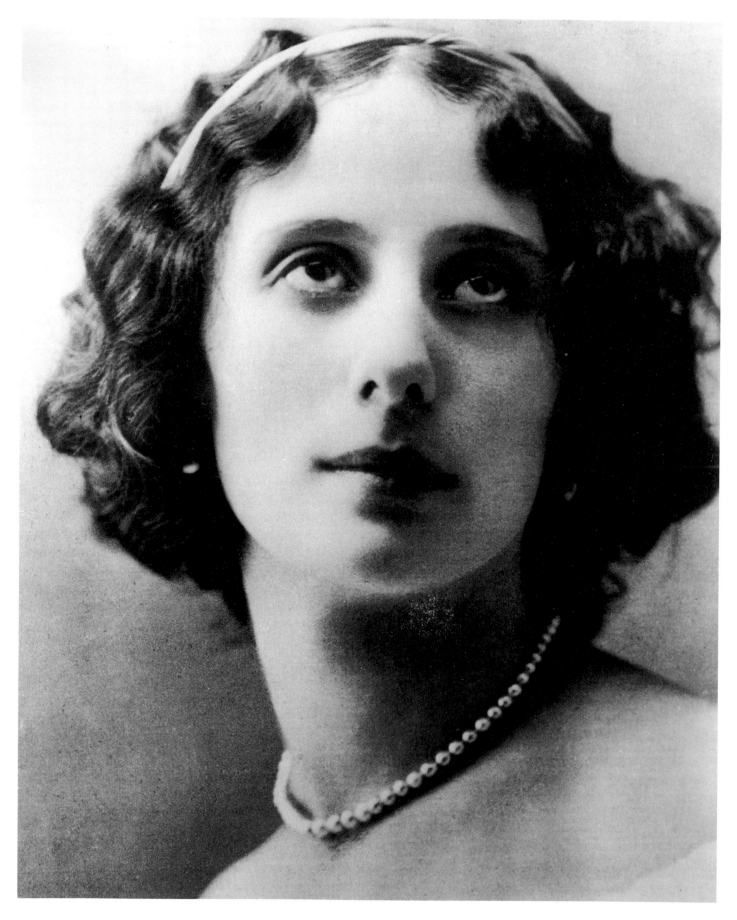

'Sadness overlays my emotion like fog upon St Petersburg.'

We Russians are not a happy people. We reflect the nature of our country, a bleak, wide land with a climate fierce and savage. In St Petersburg we have at least seven months of winter. Some winters we have only two or three sunny days a month. Everything I do must be tinctured with melancholy. I cannot eradicate it from my art because it is a vital part of my being. I am always seeing the end of things and that makes me sad. ... To those who watch closely it shows in my dancing.

The ballet critic Valerian Svetlov noted the curious fact that death was a constantly recurring theme in Pavlova's dances.

Her fame began with the mystical image of death in *Giselle. The Dying Swan* is another sad, disturbing picture of dying. ... This pure, transparent 'white death' used to move the audience to tears. *Autumn Leaves*, produced by Pavlova and by far her favourite, contained the whole psychology of her creative work and the prophecy of her tragic fate.

Yet Pavlova was by no means a tragic figure. On the contrary, she could find gaiety in everything – even the English weather.

Here in England people come to me on a cold, rainy day and they say, 'Oh, I am so sad today because it is rainy and cold!' But I am never so happy as when the rain is beating on the windows and the sky is covered with clouds. ... I am a Slav, and I think that all Slavs are like that.

This is how Pavlova the Slav impressed an English journalist in 1924.

When you talk to her you forget everything but her eyes. They are large ... and mysterious. ... They intrigue, they excite, they fascinate! You feel that they hide a wilderness of wonderful secrets. They are the eyes of a dreamer, a poet, an artiste.

When Pavlova tells you that no dancer can succeed who thinks only of success, you look into her eyes and you know that ... she is telling you the truth as her own life and experience have taught it to her. When she speaks with enthusiasm of her art, extolling it as the most beautiful and at the same time the most complex of all the arts, again you look into her eyes to discover the flashing fervour of the fanatic. ...

While she talked ... I realized the great gulf that separates the matter-of-fact Englishman from the subtle, sensitive Slav, a gulf so wide that complete understanding is practically hopeless.

Autumn Leaves.

Pavlova was full of Slavic contradictions, one minute happy in her sadness, and the next happy, like a child, in her happiness.

This is so well illustrated in a Russian article published in January 1913, which begins: 'Our pride, the world-famous ballerina, the great Pavlova, returned to St Petersburg yesterday. Slender, delicate and tiny, Pavlova looks as if she had just left school.'

With what joy I am seized when I return to my country after a long separation. It was just the same when I was a child and returned to school after the holidays. Everything was so familiar, so dear to me. I was happy to kiss every chair, every bench. . . .

When I came back to the company this time, how gay I felt. Out of habit I say 'vy' to the older ones, and they say 'ty' to me. The rehearsal room is so very, very familiar. It's as if I had never been away! The same old ballets are being staged at the Maryinsky, with the same antiquated scenery and costumes that we Russians abroad have left far behind.

I'm looking forward to my holiday – I'm going to see a new production of *The Humpbacked Horse*. It's not often that I'm a spectator of ballet . . . I am like a little girl again, trembling with impatience to see a ballet performance at the Maryinsky.

I shall stay in St Petersburg until Lent, and then I am going to Paris to open Astruc's new opera house in the Champs Elysées. . . .

After Paris I shall go 'home' to London, to my swans, for three and a half months. I shall return to the Maryinsky in September and then – how awful! – I have to go to America. . . . Oh, how I don't want to sign that contract! But I shall have to sign, for the conditions are splendid.

Incidentally, I've already amassed a fortune. I could retire tomorrow if I wanted. But I have no intention of doing that: my expenses are ludicrous, and, anyway, living abroad costs a great deal of money.

Besides, when I am doing such hard labour, I need my little comforts.

Ah, yes, don't we all know that feeling!

Above As Nikya in *La Bayadère*, the ballet in which Pavlova made her last appearance at the Maryinsky in 1913.

Opposite An early St Petersburg portrait.

The Volcano

As she had said in St Petersburg, Pavlova was back with her swans in London in time for yet another of her long seasons at the Palace Theatre.

Not only did her mere presence create excitement in the theatre but the volatile nature of everyone concerned with Russian ballet both fascinated and mystified the rest of the world

In even the best of performances many little things go wrong but the public is not aware of them. For the artist involved they are a source of fleeting anxieties and create that tension which paradoxically must exist in a theatre performance, otherwise it is flat and dull. But there are times when the tensions mount up to excess. As Pavlova, who was known to have a quick temper, once remarked:

We are all of us latent volcanoes, and unless we get a chance to use the surplus energy – well, someone is going to meet a volcano in eruption every now and then.

That is probably the best explanation of an incident reported in the London papers in the summer of 1913.

The blow on the shoulder which she administered to Novikoff Thursday night on the stage of the Palace Theatre will have a sequel similar to that which followed her quarrel with Mordkin two years ago.

Novikoff explains the incident by saying that he intended to appear with Pavlova in the United States after a . . . tour in Germany, but he told her recently that . . . his physicians had ordered him to take a long rest.

Pavlova, whose nerves he said are highly strung, was incensed at the information and slapped his face. She did not allow her anger to cool even on the stage.*

He . . . with due dignity and very nice feeling, held his peace and retired. Nobody knows why she slapped him and nobody cares. It is her way, and the daughters of the gods are privileged.

Pavlova was indeed becoming a goddess and she responded fittingly to the adoration accorded her. Here is an account of her taking her curtain calls at the Palace Theatre.

At the end of the evening the stage was lined with great trophies of flowers. A man had been handing them across the footlights in every interval. Then the applause settled into a long, unending cheer, and a dozen times at least she reappeared, bowed, kissed her hands, looked unutterable things, and retired. At last she came forward once more, stood in the centre of the stage for a few moments, so still that the house, too, became still. Then across the silence came a voice: 'Ladies and gentlemen, thank you very much. *Au revoir!*' and bowing low again and with her hands upon her heart, she withdrew, and we saw her no more. The theatre darkened for the cinematograph, but the audience shouted that they did not want it, so up went the lights again, the band played 'God Save the King', and out we came into the night.

After that, those who wanted to see her 'in the life' went round to the back of the theatre to wait.

Pavlova's car would be drawn up in front of the stage door, and a crowd would surround it, patiently waiting till she had held court in her dressing-room and changed her make-up and clothes. The first sign of life would be that the chauffeur would light the interior of the car: this would produce a buzz of anticipation. Then came a procession bearing flowers, and the car was lined with Pavlova's bouquets. Next, the people who were going to sup with her . . . came out and took their places in the car. Lastly Pavlova appeared.

Exquisite and birdlike creature, she would be draped in a wide stole of ermine or sable which fell right to the ground. She wore no jewels, but always carried one superb bouquet. Nobody dreamed of daring to ask for her autograph, any more than they would ask royalty. She paused for a moment on the doorstep, then, amid a murmur of adoration, got into the car.

Now the windows were lowered, and everyone had a final picture of the goddess, shining among flowers. She broke roses and carnations off her bouquet and threw them out to the happy crowd; and continued to do so as, very gently, almost imperceptibly, the perfumed and illuminated shrine moved away into the night.

Above With Novikoff in *Bacchanale*, 1913. *Below* Pavlova surrounded by roses.

The year 1913 was a fateful one for Pavlova. It was then that she decided to cut her ties with the Imperial Ballet and make the whole world her home until the day when she could say, 'I have performed my missionary — no, what you call, mission, and now I must rest.' But she never did rest. The manner in which she took her departure from the Maryinsky was reported in the New York Sun *– perhaps embroidered a little.*

Anna Pavlova, native of St Petersburg . . . is back in her country by adoption and her house by purchase, for the famous dancer is a voluntary exile from Russia and will live in England.

Pavlova's renunciation of Russia in favor of England, only recently made known, means a financial loss in a way. . . . Members of the Imperial Russian Ballet get an income from the state and after they are retired they are pensioned for life. . . . Still, Pavlova can manage to pull through without the pension. Her pay for dancing outside of Russia is an income for a queen, which she is – queen of the dance. . . .

The Tsar first learned of Pavlova's intention to quit Russia when she was in St Petersburg a short time ago. . . . She danced seven times in St Petersburg, and the Tsar attended nearly every performance. Twice he sent for her to come to the royal box. Both times he complimented her highly. The second time he asked why she had chosen to live outside his realm.

Pavlova described her London home, its gardens with roses and lilies of the valley and orchids, her lake with swans, her parrots, doves, thoroughbred dogs, and told of her fondness for the English, winding up her list of reasons by saying, 'And, besides, it always rains or snows in St Petersburg.'

The Tsar replied that he had understood that the sun seldom shone in London. Pavlova assured him that it peeked out there oftener than in St Petersburg. So the Tsar graciously surrendered further argument, but told Pavlova he would still expect her to return to Russia to dance and that she would retain her title as *première danseuse étoile* of the Imperial Ballet.

How strange it was that Pavlova had made all her preparations for a future that neither she nor anyone else could possibly have foreseen. She was honoured and respected in Russia but free of all commitments, and she had her home base in London ready for the formation of her own permanent company. Of course, she expected to revisit Russia from time to time, but that was her only miscalculation. As it turned out, she gave her last performance there in the summer of 1914, and after that she never saw her country again.

In the garden at Ivy House, 1913.

Pavlova gave her last performance in Russia at Pavlovsk, a few miles from St Petersburg (*above*).
Below The advertisement for that performance, 7 June 1914.

Pavlova with Marcel Bergé, St Petersburg, summer 1914.

Pavlova's life and career apparently ran smoothly until 1914, when the outbreak of war disrupted everything. She had a curious premonition of the war in an incident she described herself on many occasions later.

Before the Great War I used to have a season in Berlin every year, and, in fact, was dancing there in 1914.⋆

In Brunswick I danced at the gala performance to celebrate the christening of the Kaiser's first grandson. Not a moment's delay was permitted any artist, and the conductor was severely reprimanded for daring to wipe his glasses during the performance!

The strict, tense atmosphere, coupled with the fact that it was not considered decorous to applaud, perhaps accounts for the incident remaining in my memory as the most trying in my career. But the Kaiser himself was the first to break into applause, and then the audience followed like a tornado of clapping let loose.

I was summoned to the Royal Box; the scene lives like a cameo in my mind – the Kaiser sitting proudly upright to the left, and the Kaiserin extending to me her slim, gloved hand. To my horror I noticed the imprint of my rouged lips on the glove!

Less than three months later my country and hers were steeped in blood and war.

Left Pavlova in *Invitation to the Dance* and (*below*) with Novikoff in *The Magic Flute*, the ballets she danced for the Kaiser.

Pavlova in Berlin, 1914.

III

I have many friends lost in the war . . . and often when I must dance I am sad. Tonight I have a letter from a dear friend in London. Her husband is just killed in the war. He, too, was my friend. But one must think of the people out in front, so that you do not make them sad, too, is it not so?

It was very typical of Pavlova to put her thought for the public before her personal sorrow. Her horror at the catastrophe of war was intense and her compassion overwhelming. Wherever she went she gave special performances in aid of every kind of charity – for the wounded, for widows, for orphans, for the poor at Christmas, for the hungry and the homeless of every nationality.

But never did she feel her contribution was adequate: 'I can offer nothing but my art. It is a poor thing when such brave deeds are being done.'

AN APPEAL

BY

ANNA PAVLOWA

At this tragic moment of our existence, my heart longs to express its sympathy and be of service to suffering humanity, to help the bereft women and children of Europe, and those who are laying down their lives for their country.

I can offer nothing but my art. It is a poor thing when such brave deeds are being done, yet if you will all help me, I will do my utmost, give the best that is in me to ease the terrible suffering of our brave brothers.

New York City, October 27th, 1914

Pavlova danced *The Fairy Doll* (*top*) for the benefit of the American Red Cross in 1914.

With her little band of dancers, Pavlova had reached America during the early months of the war. She had been in Berlin at the outbreak but managed to get to England on one of the last boats to make the Channel crossing. Then she gathered her company and productions and sailed to New York, with no idea of what the future would hold for them all. It was the beginning of the most difficult years of her career, for, although she was at the height of her powers, she now had to be responsible for the members of her company as well. After two seasons of touring the continent it wasn't feasible to re-cover the same ground indefinitely; nor would she risk for her company the danger, from submarines, of a return voyage to Europe. Another solution had to be found.

At that moment she had an opportunity to buy all the productions of the bankrupt Boston Opera, and the idea of directing an opera company in conjunction with her own troupe was tremendously attractive. But first she had to raise enough money.

Pavlova was by now a great star, and her name synonymous with all that was artistic and beautiful. In addition she had a strong dramatic command in the theatre, so it isn't surprising that the movie moguls of Hollywood sought her out, in 1915, to make a spectacular epic of 'The Dumb Girl of Portici'. Financially the offer came at just the right time and the role of Fenella, which was more acting than dancing, was familiar to Pavlova from Auber's opera from which the story was adapted. Nevertheless, she was nervous of working in a new medium.

I was not over-anxious to go into pictures, and ... I stipulated that if I did consent to make a screen debut it would have to be as the dumb girl of Portici....

Just what arrangements I made financially I do not think is of interest to the public. When the documents had been signed and the date agreed upon as to when my work should begin, I began to feel somewhat nervous and apprehensive as to how I should look in pictures. So I bought a camera and spent some of my idle time in the country, where I had some of the members of my company take various photographs of me in different poses. Some of these were quite satisfactory; some were quite otherwise.

On the set of 'The Dumb Girl of Portici' with one of the rats used in the film.

'Pavlova is not a woman – she is an experience. As "The Dumb Girl of Portici" ... you may not like her at first, but slowly and surely she will crawl into your heart and almost break it when at last you see her soul winging through the clouds and almost hear her whisper – "Do you remember?"'

In his biography of Pavlova, Victor Dandré gives this interesting account of the making of the movie and of Pavlova's fears about filming her dancing.

The taking of this picture caused her much annoyance and many disappointments. From the very beginning of her career she had been accustomed to treat her art with great respect, paying close attention to every detail . . . and here she felt herself completely inexperienced and helpless. . . . Finally she insisted upon seeing the results of the first pictures and when she did so, came at once to the conclusion that it was all very bad. The make-up, apparently, was not the only thing that was wrong, for being ignorant of cinematograph camera requirements, she found that some of her movements were too pronounced, too rapid and too jerky. Eventually, other artists playing important parts, seeing her distress, and out of their affection for her, came to her aid. . . .

She was firmly convinced that, not having pronounced features, she was not 'photogenic' and that, in addition, the screen cannot reproduce dance in all its beauty. With reference to this, she used to say that she would rather her name remained a legend for future generations, than that an imperfect reproduction should lead to disappointment.

She would argue – 'Think if we, to whom Taglioni is an ideal and the summit of art, should see her on the screen, and because of the imperfections of reproduction, should exclaim: "What, is this Taglioni?"'

How lucky to have been Taglioni, not even photographed in ballet costume and missing the motion picture age completely! In no way can her legend ever be tarnished.

Pavlova did in fact film a few of her dances later in the 1920s, but she was not happy with them. From the viewpoint of ballet technique, based on the principle of legs 'turned out' from the hip, Pavlova was amazingly 'turned in'. Very possibly she didn't realise just how much until she saw those films. In any case it didn't matter because she had so adapted her dancing to her abilities that she made virtues out of everything she did, and there are some technicalities in those brief dances which no dancer today could equal.

'The Dumb Girl of Portici' had mixed reviews but Pavlova was nevertheless generally acclaimed.

With the fortune she earned in making 'The Blind Girl of Portici' [sic] for Universal, she went out one day and purchased the Boston Grand Opera Company. Truly a lady of courage and enterprise.

So said the Los Angeles Times. *Pavlova simply said:*

I thought it would be a beautiful thing for the grand opera and the dancing to go together, as in France.⋆
I want to give Americans the best that is in me, and by having an opera company to work with, my opportunities are broadened. There are many works which combine mime and ballet with opera and drama, and these I want to present. You see, the combination of the two will aid in a proper appreciation of dancing and its great value as a form of human expression. The music, the words, the plot of an opera are all reflected in the ballet, and will help to make clear what the dancing means.

Presenting and touring the Boston Grand Opera Company with the Pavlova Imperial Ballet Russe was an enterprise to make hardened impresarios tremble. It was here that Pavlova showed her Diaghilev spirit in personally directing such an ambitious project, and perhaps if it had not been in the middle of the war she would have succeeded. Alas, after nine months the venture disintegrated in financial ruin, but one can tell that Pavlova derived satisfaction from having made the attempt.

I am gratified at the many opinions expressed that ours has been the best operatic effort ever made in Boston. . . .
Whatever may be the ultimate result, it shall ever be a source of great pride to me that it is generally acknowledged that we have maintained the highest artistic ideals, and I am happy in the belief that our sacrifices have not been entirely in vain.

So Pavlova was faced with balancing practicalities against artistic ideals. She tried to have both at once by accepting a long engagement at the Hippodrome in New York – a huge variety theatre – and presenting there a version of The Sleeping Beauty, *lavishly designed by Léon Bakst.*

In Carmen, 1915.

Bakst's design for a programme page, New York Hippodrome, 1916.

At the Hippodrome Pavlova settled down to two shows a day for five months, using her spare time – what spare time? – to prepare new productions for future tours. She said, 'I should be actually unhappy if I were not adding constantly to my repertoire. That is what keeps a dancer young, I think.'

The impresario Sol Hurok described the show and his first impressions of Pavlova at supper afterwards.

I remember that ... production. It was called 'The Big Show' and it was BIG. There were Power's elephants, Mooney's horses, a trained lion act. Then came Pavlova in *The Sleeping Beauty* with Bakst's settings. And after Pavlova came the Mammoth Minstrel Show with a cast of 400 – count 'em – 400. Oh, the dear, dead, wonderful Hippodrome! ...

We went to Palisades Park and sat at a table in the outdoor restaurant. I have always known how to enjoy my food, but that night it lay almost untouched before me, and several times Madame reminded me that I was forgetting to eat.

She surprised me. I was astonished to see how much she ate, for one thing. I had eaten with tenors and sopranos, and their consumption had not startled me by its quantity. ...

Since that night ... I have supped with ballerinas more times than I can remember, and I do not even blink at the thick steaks, the mountains of potatoes, the quarts of milk they can put away. ...

But to see the delicate, fragile Pavlova, whose waist I could span with the fingers of my two hands, attack that two-inch steak made me gasp.

And as she ate and talked and laughed, I could not take my eyes from her face. The exquisite mask of the ballerina was gone; here was a woman! The cold, chiselled melancholy turned to sparkling animation, the great dark eyes shone, and every now and then the curved lips parted and there came forth a burst of rich, hearty laughter. ...

Anna Pavlova was a woman, with all of a woman's warmth and love of life, with a capacity for gaiety and adventure that could exhaust even my boundless energies. Despite the severity of her training in the Imperial School ..., despite the strictness of her devotion to her work, there was nothing nun-like about her. She loved life and she should have lived it fully, if she had not been a slave to her gifts.

Opposite As Aurora in *The Sleeping Beauty*, New York, 1916. *Below* Pavlova rehearsing *The Sleeping Beauty* with Alexander Volinine and, left to right, Theodore Stier, Alexander Smallens and ballet-master Ivan Clustine.

Pavlova with Victor Dandré.

Opposite A publicity photograph, New York, 1917 –
'piquante, pretty, slightly wistful'.

Pavlova herself almost echoed those words of Sol Hurok.

With such strict training it was impossible for the students at the Imperial School to take life other than reverently. The greatest simplicity, the most old-fashioned ideals were instilled into us. . . . Many of the artists intermarried, until the school became actually almost one family. And we married for keeps. The years that I have been Victor Dandré's wife will attest to that.

Now we come to a small enigma. I personally believe that she was sincerely expressing her principles in that last phrase. On the other hand, no one has ever been able to trace a marriage certificate in any country and Pavlova said often that she believed an artist should not marry.

Victor Dandré had left Russia with her when they went to London and he managed her company till the end. On occasion she referred to herself as Madame Dandré and, whether or not they were legally married, he was her mainstay in life – of that there seems no doubt.

Sol Hurok claimed that for press purposes in America he announced her marriage to Dandré in 1924. The following amusingly non-commital interview resulted.

'For an artist there is no husband. Pavlova, the dancer, and Pavlova, the wife, they are two very different persons. And so I keep them separate. My dancing belongs to the world, but my husband only to myself.'

This was Pavlova's casual announcement today to an astonished world that she has recently married. . . .

With a gesture of her slender hand she waved aside the blond and stalwart husband in question, insisting that to the public which knows 'Pavlova the dancer' a husband is of little consequence.

Pavlova, known to the world as 'The Incomparable' . . . is astonishingly small and slender. Her mobile, vivid face is piquante, pretty, slightly wistful. She dresses with chic stylishness and wears highly effective sports clothes. Her only jewelry was a set of rare jade earrings and bracelet.

'The world,' says Pavlova, 'likes to think of an artist as an illusion, a being of imagination and romance. When such prosaic things as husbands and other details of private life are revealed, the artist loses some of the glamour which existed before. That is why I . . . keep my private life to myself. That is why I did not tell the whole world that I was married. It is something – too intimate, perhaps – to advertise.'

In January 1917 Pavlova reached the end of her long stint with the elephants and minstrels at the Hippodrome in New York.

I am young and have not seen the whole world yet. ... It has been five years since I first danced in America, and I am no longer a novelty here. So I must move on. South America, Australia, Italy, Spain have never seen me, and if I should dance five years in each of these, then I would be an old lady.

Actually it was seven years, but five sounded much better! And with those words she blithely set off for Latin America.

During the war we were kept almost as prisoners in South America for two years. It was, if you like, a triumphant tour, but, nevertheless, it lasted too long. There were no means of getting away unless we were prepared to shed members of the company in every country.

The passport regulations were particularly onerous

Sailing to Cuba, 1917.

for us. There are dancers with me of many nationalities, so that it became almost impossible to move about.

At any rate, we had to confine our wanderings to South America.

Cuba was their first stop in Latin America and Pavlova has left a charming reminiscence of the theatre.

They would have been rehearsing on the stage and she may have stayed on later than the others – trying on her ballet shoes? – anyway, she was able, through the stage manager's peep-hole in the curtain, to observe the wooden dance floor that must have been placed over the stalls' seating area.

The most magnificent theatre I can remember is the National Opera in Havana. It is the private property of a club; a beautiful white granite building rather reminding one of a stately Venetian palace. In addition to the large and beautiful theatre it accommodates the club members with every imaginable convenience and luxury. ...

The night after our arrival there, there was one of those public balls to which anybody could go for the price. There seemed to be no colour line, and I was told that the throng of dancers included all strata of society from the demi-monde to the nobility, although of the latter there were only males.

I ventured on the stage where we were to begin our season two nights later, and through the curtains saw this strange sight without being myself seen. The floor was so completely filled that couples were elbow to elbow and back to back, so close that dancing as we know it was impossible. What they did was a sort of wriggle with the feet, scarcely moving more than an inch with each step. When some couple would elaborate on this with something original, spectators in the boxes felt privileged to shout approval to them, as they would to an artist on the stage.

There were two bands, one on either side of the top tier, and what they played was the most elemental jazz I have heard. Imagine converting a Liszt Hungarian Rhapsody into syncopation. That was one of their favourites, but they also jazzed Chopin, Tchaikovsky, Saint-Saëns and other classic composers.

FOLIO *288*   CUARTO No. *220/21*

HOTEL INGLATERRA
HAVANA

Hijos de Felipe González, S. en C.
PROPIETARIOS

HABANA, CUBA *15/3/917*

Sr. *Anna Pavlowa*

DEBE:

			U. S. CURRENCY	
Días Habitación	3	Days Room only	54	.
Restaurant		Restaurant	2	60
Lavado		Laundry bill		
Expreso		Express		
Cables			10	90
		Bill rendered	175	29
			242	79
		Restaurant	3	.
			243	09

Imp. Obrapía 99

NOTA:—Las cuentas deben ser pagadas los Lunes.
NOTE:—Bills most be payable Mondays.

At the Hotel Inglaterra, Havana, 'bills most be payable Mondays.'

The hazards of Latin American politics gave Pavlova an unexpected chance to dance for the really poor people of Mexico City. She always loved the general public, and the more general the better.

In Mexico a magnificent national theatre is being built. I had hoped that it would be ready for my visit but the revolution held everything up.

There is a huge bull-fighting ring there capable of seating 30,000 people. Rather than cancel my engagement I arranged to appear there in the open air to the largest audience, I think, before which any dancer has appeared.⋆

A dancing platform was placed in the end of the bullring for me, with the orchestra close by. It was a glorious afternoon, but hot! The wonderful sunshine, the glorious blue sky without a single cloud – I can see it now in fancy. But it *was* hot, I must admit, for dancing.

It was a wonderful experience, dancing to a very mixed audience, among whom were a large sprinkling of Indians. Their enthusiasm at the end was unbounded: they chanted their own weird songs and made extraordinary noises before they would let me go.

Some of the Mexicans, carried away apparently by the rhythm of the music and the dance, shouted with excitement and threw their sombreros at my feet. When a Mexican gives you his sombrero, it is like an Englishwoman giving you her pearls.

Her musical director, Theodore Stier, who not long before had been conducting the orchestra at an open-air theatre with the music librarian holding an umbrella over his head, takes up Pavlova's story of the bullring in Mexico.

At the second performance it rained.

Pavlova carried on ... for as long as it remained possible for her to do so. Longer, in fact, than was safe.... For the sake of all concerned it was absolutely necessary to ring down the curtain after the performance had lasted only a very short time indeed.

And then there was trouble with a capital T....

To continue the performance was impossible. To satisfy the house that this was so was a greater impossibility still. Eventually it was represented to us by the management ... that the stage door still stood where it did, and that if we were wise we should employ that exit while the going remained good.

Which we did.

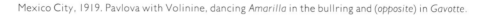

Mexico City, 1919. Pavlova with Volinine, dancing *Amarilla* in the bullring and (*opposite*) in *Gavotte*.

Invitation to the Dance, Lima, 1917.

Almost everything to do with the Latin-American tour was uncertain; bookings were made as they went along, so no one ever knew what their movements would be for more than a couple of months ahead — and occasionally the company ran close to bankruptcy. But through it all Pavlova never failed to be engagingly fresh and enthusiastic when she spoke with the press.

Such an instance was in Buenos Aires in 1917.

Ah, but it has been a happy tour in South America. . . . The countries have been so interesting. There has been so much to see and do, and the people have been so kind. We were in Havana in February, on the first day of the Cuban revolution, and that was interesting, although it made us late. Then we went to Costa Rica, where there were so many nice people, and afterwards to Panama and Guayaquil. It is hard work performing in these tropical countries, and there are other difficulties, theatres, organization, but the people were all so kind.

André Olivéroff was one of the dancers with Pavlova in the 102° heat of Guayaquil, where rehearsals and matinée performances took place relentlessly as though the company was in London or Paris instead of almost on the equator. They had arrived by cattle boat; most of the dancers had slept on deck rather than in the sweltering, over-crowded cabins, and Pavlova had been especially horrified by the intermittent moanings of the doomed cattle in the hold of the ship. Olivéroff gives this picture of Pavlova under the most adverse conditions.

Once the novelty of Guayaquil had worn off, there was little to occupy our idle hours, save our ever-present consciousness of the staggering heat. By the end of the first week, it seemed we had been there for ever. . . . Our work became a concentrated form of punishment. Madame alone, with her mysterious recourse to a source of power which was shut off from mere human beings, managed, in public anyway, to triumph over conditions which extinguished the spark of life in the rest of us. If you like, you may call this 'mysterious power' her steadfast will, or her physical endurance. Personally, I could never quite account for it by these phrases.

This mysterious power sustained her through everything. Arrival in any new city was a source of exhilaration, no matter what the journey to get there. Here she is again in Buenos Aires.

The sitting-room of her suite had been turned into a reception room and although it was only ten o'clock on the morning following a tiresome two days' journey across the continent (and the dust of Argentina's pampas had given her a slight cold), there were half a dozen people claiming her attention, her telephone bell was ringing every few seconds, and Madame's bull terrier ('He gives me much trouble') was endeavouring to size me up. . . .

Into a room bright with great bunches of flowers and looking out over the muddy waters of the River Plate, looking somewhat less muddy in the bright sunshine of the morning, Pavlova had come quietly and graciously, dressed in a simple costume of white. . . . She sat on a sofa during her talk, her hands moving to illustrate her words and her face lighting up with the memories those words recalled. . . .

'We went . . . to Lima, where we had very great success, a reception like we should have in Russia. And at Valparaiso it was wonderful — twenty-four performances one after the other. Then to Santiago, where I was surprised to see how beautiful the city is, and how big its theatres. And now we are in Buenos Aires, where we hope to stop about a month.

And then to Brazil. But after that I do not know. The war makes things so difficult. We would all like to go back to Russia after having been away so long. But it is even more trouble getting back to Russia than it is to England. . . . But the war — I do not know. It is terrible, so much suffering — everything turned upside down. I am glad to be for a time in a quiet country where there is no war. Our art helps us to forget: in art one has to forget — you understand?'

The war was finally over and with many delays Pavlova got back to Europe after an absence of five years. She found a vastly changed world. An English journalist talked to her in the bleak surroundings of an empty stage during a rehearsal in Paris, and the article appeared under the heading 'The Sadness of Pavlova' in The Observer *in June 1921.*

It was in the vast empty vessel of the Trocadero, the biggest hall in Paris, that Anna Pavlova told me something of her experiences and her intentions. Long black draperies were being placed in position by workmen. In one corner a muscular member of what Pavlova calls her family was going through gymnastic exercises. . . . Two or three girls with only the remotest resemblance to a Degas picture were testing the suppleness of their limbs and executing now and again some graceful steps and gestures. The conductor of the orchestra, clad in a sweater, was addressing his final injunctions to a crowd of musicians gathered round him. . . . It was all desultory and haphazard, and the unoccupied sweep of stalls and gilded balconies looked dismal as a mausoleum. . . .

'Soon I hope to be back in London,' she told me. . . . 'That will give me great pleasure, for the English people are so appreciative. It means so much – appreciation. I do not think it is realized how hard it is for an artist to produce of the best in these days of trouble. How can one give oneself in these times of uncertainty and distress? And without that absolute giving of oneself there is no real art.'

With great earnestness did she make that simple utterance, spreading her hands in the gesture of giving. After all, what better definition of art in any form than this definition of self-giving? 'But, oh!' she cried sadly, 'how depressed one is sometimes tempted to be in a storm-tossed world! And how fatal depression must be to those who wish to put their soul into their work!'

I asked her if she did not think that there was a greater demand than ever for the dance, precisely as the result of the tremendous and pent-up emotions of the past few years. . . .

In her admirable French, broken now and again by a word of English, she accepted . . . this present need for . . . the dance. But she could not forget the spiritual difficulties while the material circumstances are so hard – harder than they have been, in the experience of Pavlova, at any moment except during the war. . . .

'Not for two or three years do I expect they will really improve,' she said, 'and although I am grateful for the reception which is everywhere accorded me it is not yet easy to travel and look after my large family. Certainly . . . it was worse during the war.

'These things must and do affect one's art. They make one very sad sometimes. . . . But I am trying to do what I can for I think my art is needed.'

We talked about a matter about which everybody in Paris is talking – the impending departure of Isadora Duncan, that other great artist, for Moscow. . . . I repeated to Anna Pavlova, who listened eagerly, her thin pure face with the big burning eyes and the dark flattened hair parted over the broad brow bent towards me, what Isadora Duncan had said a few days before. That this American exponent of the dance – how different is her method from the method of Pavlova, and how different her majestic beauty from the sylph-like beauty of Pavlova, and yet how essentially similar their genius – should be going to her own country, now struggling in deeper adversity than any Western country, interested her greatly. Isadora Duncan complained that when she gave a spectacle at Paris the expenses and the taxes were so high that she was compelled to raise abnormally the price of places.

What has tempted her to go to Russia is that Lounatcharsky has offered her a *salle*, and has offered to help her to teach her pupils under the protection of the government. She goes to Russia with the hope of founding a great popular theatre.

The sympathy of Pavlova was expressed in unmistakable terms. But the same melancholy as had tinged the whole conversation again appeared. . . . Pavlova, too, is thinking of the Russian children, and proposes to devote the proceeds of these Paris representations to the poor infants of exiled Russians, and to found a charitable fund which will . . . bear her name.

Pavlova adored children, but lacked that fulfilment in her life. In 1921 she was forty, a mature, compassionate woman. Sometimes she said she would like to have a baby – 'but it does not go with my art'. So she reared to maturity a group of refugee girls, which cost a lot of money.

THE ANNA PAVLOVA FOUNDATION
SPECIAL MATINEE
Thursday, October 2nd, at 2.30 p.m.

Madame PAVLOVA is devoting the whole of her proceeds to the Refugee Home.

PRICES AS USUAL

During the year 1921, when in Paris, the worst hardships I witnessed were those endured by the little Russian children, some without homes, many actually starving—little refugees of my own land mutely pleading for help in a strange country. Something had to be done at once, so at St. Cloud, near Paris, I rented for some of them a suitable home, where they now live in happiness and are well cared for. That little band is ever increasing; already it has assumed proportions beyond my private purse to entirely support.

I am most anxious to continue this work—**will you please help me ?**

Above An appeal for her Paris Refugee Home printed in a Covent Garden programme in the twenties.

Below Visiting a children's home during her 1911 provincial tour of England.

Sailing to Japan on the *Empress of Canada*, September 1922.

One begins to feel that the only sustenance Pavlova needed in these later years was the response of people – all people – to her dancing.

I feel that, if I were ever quite satisfied, any power I possess would leave me. It is the divine discontent that drives us artists always onward. People wonder why we are never at rest. Remember, we surrender the things that others find so beautiful – the divine wonder of real home life, the quiet growth with and for one's surroundings – but it is because ambition will not let us rest. I do not excuse myself of that feeling – without it the world would lose much that is best of the intangible things that its restless artists give it. . . .

The East had always fascinated me. One of the greatest ambitions remaining to me was to subjugate the Orient to my art, proving its power over people of any race or color.

Having criss-crossed the Western world so many times, Pavlova wanted fresh inspiration, and this she found in her tours of the East.

Japan exceeded all her expectations: beauty surrounded her everywhere from the moment the company arrived in Yokohama. Pavlova was thrilled. She said, 'There is nothing in this country that one wants to throw away.'

Below Arriving in Yokohama. *Above* Pavlova being greeted by Japanese dancers.

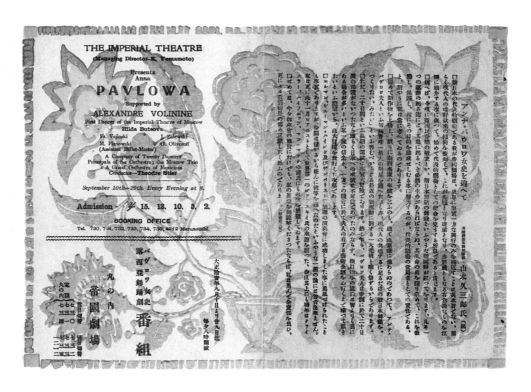

Pavlova souvenir programme, Imperial Theatre, Tokyo, 1922.

Opposite With Japanese actor Kikugoro and family.

In Japan, where I have given performances in eleven cities, the theatres in the interior are rather strange to our Western ideas, for there are no seats as in our theatres. The audience sits each on a small square of wood and wicker, which is only a few inches high, and that is why one has the impression that everyone is sitting on the floor. The only theatre of European model we found was the Imperial in Tokyo, and this was almost the only building left intact after the earthquake and fire which happened a year after we were there. . . .

I was rather surprised that they showed such an interest in hearing about England, and several people whom I met questioned me about George Bernard Shaw.★

They did understand much of our performances, and asked numerous naive questions about the rest of them. With synopses printed in Japanese, they enjoyed fully those ballets in which a story is told, like *Autumn Leaves*, *The Fairy Doll* and *Amarilla*, but were not so quick to grasp *Chopiniana*, which is simply a series of classical dances to Chopin's music. . . . They inclined to look for some pantomime meaning in the various movements and the tarlatan skirts.

Accounts of audience appreciation given by company members are contradictory and most confusing. Molly Lake made this comment on the audiences:

The Japanese take their pleasures very stoically, and their features betray no trace of whether they are pleased or the reverse. They applaud by hand claps, and a peculiar sibilant intaking of the breath through closed teeth.

Talking of the Tokyo performances, Harcourt Algeranoff, who had recently joined the Pavlova company, wrote:

Whether the audience at the Imperial Theatre liked us or not we never could tell, because Japanese audiences do not applaud. It was a terrible anticlimax; we would put all our energy into a finale, the curtain would come down and nothing would happen at all, except a little discreet whispering and cigarette lighting. Fortunately the newspapers published rapturous notices or we would never have had any idea of what Russian ballet meant to Japan.

Russian Ballet in Tokyo

The only review I have of the Tokyo opening night, translated from a Japanese journal called The New Stage Art, *is bizarre in the extreme. The author, Ryunosuke Akutagawa, does explain elsewhere that he is a novelist, and knows little of Russian ballet.*

Amarilla, Chopiniana and seven dances including *The Dying Swan* were the Russian Ballet I saw.

Amarilla was disgusting. First, the scenery was unpleasant. The colour of the woods, the sky, and even the stone balustrade were impossible. Secondly, the libretto was artificial and unpleasant. The love of a beautiful gypsy girl and a count has a Watteau-like charm, one might say, but I was overwhelmed by its poisonous sweetness. If at the opera you do not like what you see, you may close your eyes, but at the ballet if you close your eyes it is a catastrophe. Thirdly, the gypsy girl of Anna Pavlova was disagreeable, exaggerated, voluptuous, hysterical even. In a word she was decadent. The society to which this art was born, the society in which such an art is admired, is, giving a favourable account, a world of sexual abnormality. I am not a moralist. ... I even have some respect for violent lust. But I do not sympathize with abnormal, feeble, disguised lust. ... As soon as the curtain fell I rushed to the foyer cursing Anna Pavlova, the Imperial Theatre, and the magazine ... that engaged me to produce an article about this performance. ...

After *Amarilla* came *Chopiniana*. I was indifferent to that, too. The impression of the stage was just like a handkerchief box or the picture of a European story book cover. Fortunately, this ballet has no story. ... Moreover, to see the dancers dressed in white and moving here and there in a bluish spotlight is a beautiful sight. Although I was indifferent, mentally I did not feel the positive unpleasantness I felt when I saw *Amarilla*. Physically, I felt dizzy a couple of times. To watch Western ballet dancers turn like tops or soar in the air is not good for one's health. ... Fortunately, I felt only dizziness, but there was a gentleman groaning under the table of the smoking-room when I went to the foyer in the intermission. He told me he was Russian-Ballet-sick – in the same way as one might be sea-sick. ...

My vitality was recovered when I saw the seven dances, which included *The Dying Swan*. Gradually, from the stage 'art' began to radiate its dim lustre as moonlight through the mist. *The Dying Swan* was beautiful – at least, more beautiful than the Japanese translation of the words 'The Dying Swan' suggests. Seeing Anna Pavlova dancing, one feels bonelessness before skill. In fact, we Japanese have never seen such a freely flexible body other than that of a boneless man; but, of course, a boneless man is grotesque. The feeling of grotesqueness remained within me; I felt nervous and ridiculous. ... However, when I saw *The Dying Swan* it was strange how the feeling of bonelessness disappeared suddenly. As I gazed upon the arms and legs of Pavlova, the neck and wings of the swan seemed to emerge, accompanied by the wake and ripple of the lake; I even heard the soundless voice – I could not believe my senses. Pavlova became magnificent. The feeling of decadence remained, but I could overlook it. I had seen something beautiful. I could not complain. Pavlova was good. ...

My impression of Russian Ballet as a whole is as follows. Russian Ballet contains a sinister vagueness, never found in *The Dying Swan*. This sinister vagueness is vivid, barbaric, full of sunlight; it smells of rye, and is very close to the Orient. It has not the powerful, accomplished form of *The Dying Swan* as yet, and it is evident in various dances from time to time. I admire *The Dying Swan* because it does not have the power to make me uneasy. I have experienced the breeze of that exquisite world alongside French poetry, but the sinister vagueness felt before lacks the delicacy of this breeze.

These formidable Russian geniuses all have this sinister vagueness in their powerful veins. Understanding Russian Ballet this way, I think it has tremendous possibilities. In retrospect, I feel I was careless to have ridiculed *Amarilla* – even if I did not like it.

Amarilla ... 'In a word she was decadent.'

From Japan the company moved on to China, which Pavlova disliked as much as she had loved Japan. The reason was an incident in a Shanghai street which gravely offended her, as Theodore Stier explained.

At that time Shanghai was at the height of its prosperity, and of all the cities in the world we visited was by far the cheapest to live in. . . . A rickshaw coolie, for instance, would take one almost any distance for a matter of ten cents. . . .

Driving home from the theatre in a rickshaw . . . the coolie demanded a fee slightly in excess of the recognised rate. He became so insistent at last that he attracted the attention of a Sikh policeman, who, without listening to a word of his explanation, hit the unfortunate coolie over the head with his baton, and left him lying insensible in the road.

That incident alone was sufficient to give Pavlova a lasting dislike to Shanghai, and, to only a lesser extent, to China in general. From that day, except for the theatre, she refused resolutely to leave her hotel.

By contrast, the revelation of Indian culture was a thrilling experience for Pavlova. The art and the dancing gave her vivid impressions that she could adapt to ballet form. But she was disappointed in the Indians' apathetic attitude to their own rich artistic heritage.

Why is there so much lack of enthusiasm in India? You have beautiful music, beautiful clothes and a beautiful sense of colour. Your poetic lore is rich with themes suitable for rhythmic interpretation. What is already beautiful can be made much more beautiful if only you bestow thought upon it. . . .

I do not want to show what I can do with your art, but what you can do yourselves. I have noticed the beauty of form and movement of Indian women. A slight movement of the body of two or three ordinary women in the street that I saw has convinced me of the presence of a latent art which I am sure can be developed and presented on the stage as an expression of true art. . . .

Our dance is choreographic; our ideas, our music, our scenes are all suited to it; but I feel sure that we can with our dance help a great deal in the interpretation of your ideas through your dance. This has been done in Egypt, in Japan, and in other countries of the East.

Pavlova arriving in Bombay on her return visit there in 1928.

Opposite Posing in the garden at Ivy House, 1923.

Wherever she went, Pavlova made a point of studying the national dances, and she often incorporated them in her productions. Theodore Stier was with her when she went to an Indian theatre to see the Nautch girls dancing for the first time.

Rarely have I seen Pavlova so impressed – far more so than she had been by a performance of the Geisha in Japan. Actually the movements of the Nautch dancers were not very dissimilar to our own. In addition, their costumes were a very miracle of loveliness. . . .

To round off this perfection, too, was the native music, which was . . . far more inspiring than any we had heard since leaving the Western world behind.

To Pavlova there was only one way fitting to mark her appreciation of all this beauty – to prepare an Indian ballet for inclusion in her own repertoire. . . . Once having come to this decision, she set to work with her usual thoroughness to prepare her plans.

Pavlova talked at length about the creation of her ballet Ajanta Frescoes *in an interview she gave later in America.*

I saw the pilgrims . . . and followed them into the cave of Ajanta. The pilgrims I have not literally produced for you. No! I wouldn't do that, and you wouldn't tolerate it. They are often perfectly terrible, the most forlorn and piteous sight in the world. Yet, inspired by faith, they come for hundreds and thousands of miles, the great and the low, the rich and the poor, they file into that cave, and sit in meditation before the image of Gautama Buddha. . . .

Inside the cave are many frescoes, and an art, dating from about the fifth century before Christ. . . .

Need I tell you that the people of the age of Buddha were, on the one hand, great philosophers and mystics. But they were not the monks that Christianity gave the world. Very far from it! And on these walls all life is seen – flowers, birds and beasts, prince and peasant, courtier and hermit, courtesan and merchant – the court, bazaar, garden, forest, palace. . . .

There one sees the conception that has gone all over the Hindu world, . . . cherished wherever the religion of Buddha enters – the scene of Buddha's renunciation. . . . Well, that is the theme of my picture, which at least as far as the decorations are concerned, and the costumes, too, is a precise reproduction of what we saw on those walls in the cave of Ajanta. . . .

But now I come to a difficulty every artist will appreciate. How could I achieve a recrudescence of all this life which has passed, never to return, and of which there is no actual, existing vestige in India today?

It is there – in this effort to revive a mighty and unrevivable past – that I know in a large measure I failed. What I have done is an enormous gratification to me, and that it is a solid accomplishment is proved to me by the expressions of leading Indian scholars . . . the world over. But it is not wholly a success, because two things had to be opposed – artistic impression and accurate archeology.

The public would have been better pleased . . . if I had shown them a bigger cave than exists, if I had painted from imagination a place of endless delight. But I could not do this and show Ajanta to the world. I copied it, in most instances quite literally, only expanding for the demands of such stages that I occupied, and in one instance contracting. . . .

Then I had to invent. I had to devise approximate dances after hints in the frescoes. I had to give Mr Tcherepnine, for his musical material, traditional Indian tunes, and tell him to stick to them. He was disappointed. He said, 'I've lived in the East. I know Ajanta, and Persia, and much of India. Let me just imagine and compose in my own way.' I replied that that could not be done. We must have music of Ajanta. I think I was wrong. I think I must let my composer do as he pleases in making me a new score – for the music is so important. You follow the music more than you know, with your ear, when you are listening with your eye.

You remember what Wilde said once? He said that one man thought he had to go to Japan to paint Japanese pictures, but another man, wiser, sat in Hyde Park and painted pictures a thousand times more Japanese than the travelled artist ever approximated. And in that there is a great nub of truth.

With Novikoff in Ajanta Frescoes, *1923.*

Pavlova made a second Indian tour only two years before her death, yet still her excitement and enthusiasm were almost childish as she received the press in her Calcutta hotel.

An endless stream of page-boys carrying huge bouquets kept up a steady tattoo along the corridor outside the door of Madame Anna Pavlova's room in the Grand Hotel, Calcutta, yesterday morning.

Opposite a door on which was tacked a card requesting silence, the callers halted. 'Madame is resting,' explained the pleasant French maid to all enquirers, and callers who had hoped to meet the great ballerina retraced their steps reluctantly. . . .

Pavlova was about to leave for rehearsal at the theatre when I called (writes a *Statesman* reporter), but she brushed aside my proposal to call again at some more convenient time with a friendly smile that put me at ease immediately. A vivid elfin creature in a bluish-grey gown of some flimsy material, she was, one felt, instinctively the most vital thing in that room half-filled with exquisite deep red roses.

'A temperament on wings – a feminine flame rather than a creature of flesh and blood' – the description fitted aptly.

'Please tell everybody how happy I am to come back to Calcutta,' were almost her first words. 'I shall never forget my first visit – never. Everyone was so kind to me,' she added with emotion.

India has completely captivated Pavlova – especially India's womanhood. 'Indian women are delightful,' she exclaimed, 'So, so . . .' 'Feminine', suggested her husband, who sat by her side. 'Yes, feminine, that's what I mean,' Pavlova responded. 'Such grace, such rhythm in their movement. The saree is the most beautiful dress in the world,' she went on enthusiastically.

'And do you know what I saw at Bombay?' she enquired tragically. I confessed my ignorance. 'I saw some lovely Indian girls in European clothes, with their dresses oh – so – so – so – terrible, terrible.' Pavlova demonstrated her disapproval with a grimace. 'Then you don't approve of the modern girl's short skirts?' I asked.

Pavlova laughed. 'Oh, sometimes,' she said, 'But not for Indian ladies. Their dress is much nicer than ours.'

The Indian critics and scholars were surprised when they saw Ajanta Frescoes *and Pavlova's second Eastern ballet,* Oriental Impressions. *They realized the extent of her achievement in so faithfully interpreting a culture very alien to her own. However, it is interesting to read Pavlova's summation of her efforts to blend East and West.*

I was particularly interested in my Eastern adventures. . . . Almost all values seemed different from ours, the theatre is strange, ideas on art quite opposite.*

Well, it has been a great experience, and this experience has determined me to do more in Indian art and the art of other countries. . . . Yet I know this: I can never do the completely truthful thing. I have faced that fact. Here are my girls. As accomplished technicians, I am sure, as you will find in any company, very faithful to their work, very enthusiastic, industrious, idealistic. They were taught dancing by Japanese and Hindus. They achieve the outside appearance of that dancing.

The inside feeling neither they nor I can wholly achieve, and we know it. It is a different consciousness that animates the dances of the East and West. Perhaps, for this very reason, it is well that we cannot be utterly Eastern. The Western audiences might not understand us. We occupy nearer a middle ground between two peoples. It is all right for our work, good for the stage, and good for art and spiritual understanding. But it is not the real Indian expression. . . .

The training is so different. . . . It is a mental, indeed, a philosophical training that the West doesn't know and certainly cannot learn quickly. And it is utterly wonderful. It has a power which I try to employ in my dances, but which I certainly could never by means of words explain. . . .

My first emotion in my work is the emotion of art. That is an emotion known only to those who have experienced it. And yet something bigger, vaster, warmer, too, surrounds that emotion, and cradles it in its depths. That is the sure feeling of joy and gratitude which I know when I put on the stage something at least relatively true of the soul of a people, and that people thank me – speaking or silent – for what is in their hearts, as, for example many people in India have thanked me for establishing even a very crude and incomplete communication between them and the Western world.

Top Krishna and Radha with Harcourt Algeranoff.
Above Design by Orest Allegri for *Hindu Wedding*. These ballets formed part of the *Oriental Impressions* trilogy.

Really, some government should subsidize me as an artistic ambassadress. For that's what I am, isn't it? This my work of being ambassadress is very hard, difficult, sometimes even dangerous, and yet it is the work which the world most needs today. I know this, though I am no student of world affairs, dislike politics, have no faith in generals or armies, or even leagues, treaties and the like. I know that when the real brotherhood of nations comes in this world – and it will come, I think, in a better day than you or I will live to see – I know that day will be supremely the day of the artist's triumph. It is the artist, and only the artist, who at last can make people understand.

I find those words profound and pray they may be prophetic. Cultural exchanges, which today are taken for granted as a means of promoting better understanding between nations, almost always include exchange visits of dance companies. Pavlova accomplished this work on her own and unsubsidized by any government.

Those who come to my performances may have – do have, in many cases – the prejudices of their insularity. (One need not dwell on an island to be insular.) They see a small fragment, as beautiful a fragment as I have been able to find and translate for them, of the life and spirit of their fellow-being on the other side of the world. They are astonished. They say, 'We never heard of this. We heard of a general, an army, a massacre, a false politician leading the deluded ones astray. We heard of their cruelties, greeds and dominances. But what is this? Can it be from that nation this wonder comes?'

They are incredulous. But, with the memory of that exotic beauty haunting them, they begin to reflect. At last the inevitable conclusion will arrive. 'The people that created this can be no enemy of mine.'

That is an inevitable realization of art. Art, understanding, love, indeed, is at the root the same thing.

Pavlova's first Eastern tour ended in Egypt in 1923.

Opposite Alexandria.

Below Cairo.

IV
___

Dancing is my gift and my life. . . . God gave me this gift to bring delight to others. That is why I was born. I am haunted by the need to dance.★

It is the same to me whether I am rehearsing in my own room at home, or on the empty darkened stage, or facing an audience across the footlights. . . .

When I dance, I am not conscious of my body. I feel I am one with the dance. It is as though I were caught up by a magical rhythm, that I am all rhythm, part of that greater rhythm which animates life itself. It is my life. I know of no other. It is the purest expression of every emotion, earthly and spiritual. It is happiness.

This is Pavlova in 1925. Her mission has now taken precedence over all else in her life. Is it, perhaps, because she knows that she will never experience the great universal relationships of wife and mother? I don't believe so. She has always been different from other mortals and, more likely, with the passing of time, has grown to accept that the true life of a woman is unrealizable for one whose fate is to serve the public till her last breath.

Pavlova made, in all, seven North American tours with her own company, appearing in never less than three numbers at each performance. Sometimes she danced in more than 150 cities during the course of a single tour.

My program in America was to visit one town each day for seven months, and cover 26,000 miles on my travels. . . .

I found the long journeys particularly tiring. Often it meant that we had to get into an express after our performance, snatch what rest we could despite the bumping and the noise, and arrive at our next destination only just in time to get changed, and appear on the stage again.⋆

During all these years of incessant globe-trotting, we naturally played in all kinds of theatres, concert halls and public places of every description. . . . In one case, I think it was Nashville, our performance actually took place in a kind of mission hall, where the audience sat in pews and I, for dressing purposes, had to climb to the organ loft. One could not help being amused by the character of our Bacchanalian dances and the somewhat biblical atmosphere of our surroundings.⋆

At Fresno, California, a fire broke out in a building in the next block while we were dancing. The electric light cable was cut by the fireman, plunging the theatre into pitch darkness, but there was no panic. Someone at the back kept the whole audience laughing with jokes . . . and before anyone had thought of leaving a procession came hurrying in with the headlights from all the cars which were standing outside. A couple of dynamos were rigged up, the rest of our performance being given in the amazingly bright light thus produced. . . .

While in America I was not immune from the terrestrial disturbances which so frequently afflict that unfortunate country. In Texas I was detained in a small town by a flood, which carried away a railway bridge. I believe every one of the six thousand inhabitants turned out to the local cinema, not to see me dance but to be intrigued with the mechanical working of the curtain and side scenery!

One of my strangest experiences in the States was having my performance banned unless I chose to wear longer ballet skirts. . . . Particularly in America was this a surprise to me, when I considered some of the plays and films that are made and shown there. The evil was in the mind of my critics, I think, rather than in the beautiful art which it has always been my endeavor to give to the world.

On the stage she was incomparable. But in everyday life the central image was that of a simple woman.

Mme Anna Pavlova, the one and only Pavlova, Pavlova the Incomparable, is just a plain, ordinary, everyday little piece of femininity – off the stage. . . . Trailing in her every step is Mme Pavlova's bulldog. That dog keeps an affectionate eye on his mistress constantly. She also is fond of the dog and the two are great pals.⋆

If one would interview Mme Pavlova and come away with anything concrete by which he might give some conception of what she said, he should take with him a motion-picture camera. . . . She speaks in swift, vivid, eloquent gestures as much as in words. . . . It is one thing to record in type that Mme Pavlova said that before they became good dancers American girls should learn good manners, and another to see her imitate the way some American girls act in the presence of their elders. A whole volume on etiquette would be puerile in comparison with that delicious bit of dumb show.⋆

Pavlova . . . was dressed with the veriest simplicity, and she talked with the lightsomeness of a schoolgirl. A jaunty tan hat of felt without ornament; a plain little dress with a rather short skirt; a chain of red beads around her neck; a red sash at her waist; any schoolgirl would have worn the same. That is the secret of Pavlova. She is genuine, and her art is genuine.⋆

Dressed in a costume of nun-like simplicity, almost severity, Madame Pavlova, found waiting her train at the Third Street depot, scarcely impressed the beholder as a woman who has won vast footlight fame. It is when you talk to her, when you see the flame of inspiration leap into her great dark eyes, when she speaks of the art that is dearer to her than life, that you realize you are in the presence of genius.

Opposite Sailing back to Europe on the *Finlandia* in March 1921 at the end of her North American tour.

The Butterfly.

Although Pavlova concentrated totally on creating beauty in her performances, she could never be completely aware of the impact she had on people because she could never see herself on the stage. Of course, she could read reviews like this one, but never, herself, experience the emotion that completely bowled over this critic from the Los Angeles Examiner.

She did one number so incomparably that it fevered the audience with joy.

I doubt that many of us among those present last night ever saw her do *The Butterfly* before. There is a stronger doubt that anyone will ever see her do it with the same degree of self merging into a butterfly again. Butterflies have souls; Pavlova proved it, for she must have seized a butterfly's very being and encompassed it with her own. It was a direct impersonation of a butterfly, floating, sipping, quivering with the joy of life; as indifferent to everything as one of those iridescent little bubbles you see ... at the bottom of the tube of a champagne glass, intoxicated with its own beauty, filled with the sunshine the grapes have absorbed. . . .

There will be two more performances. ... If Pavlova does *The Butterfly* at either, buy all the seats you can, even if you have to mortgage your automobile.

That review is so intoxicating in itself that it gives me the feeling I have just seen Pavlova dancing, and I understand completely why it was said:

Pavlova is inseparable from her art: she lives it, breathes it, dreams of the future of dancing in the world.

In many countries she talked of the possibilities for the future, but it was for America that she held the highest hopes.

Art is in no sense racial, nor does it know geographical limits; but it does have the capacity to reflect, without intrusion, national spirit. With a great nation like yours your artists would take place in the world with those of Italy, Russia, France and other countries, distinctive yet of universal quality. What America lacks is its own forms of art, its own artists. This is because of two things: your too plentiful money, and your general idea that talent and ability is genius.

No one can arrive from being talented alone. In my life I have seen them come to the front – brilliant-minded people; intense men and women who had great talent for what they did, but they did not, could not last. . . .

I worked for seven years under iron discipline, under ceaseless toil. It is so with all true artists.

God gives talent, work transforms talent into genius.

Your rich men, your Vanderbilts, your Kahns have done much; your Metropolitan and Chicago operas are wonderfully given, wonderfully sung. But what are you doing for the young Americans who wish to follow an artist's career? Nothing. They have to go to Paris, Rome or Petrograd to learn, and they come back not imbued with the spirit of their country, but with the traits and tendencies of art as interpreted by other traditions and spirit. . . .

If America had the system of conservatories and then places for their graduates, you would soon be producing artists who would have all the universal traits of art.⋆

From your American women some day will come the greatest dancer the world will ever know. From where else than this melting pot of all the nations could come an international or universal artist to best interpret all moods? Your great country will produce a superb dancer not bound by old traditions and narrow nationalism.

No other country can produce her. No other country represents every racial characteristic in the world. No other people feel the influence of nature so keenly, and nature is the greatest developer of art. Here in America you run the gamut of the seasons more than any other country. You have a tender spring, changing and unpredictable, a summer of intense, burning sunshine. You have a flaming autumn, the like of which is never seen elsewhere. And your winter can be almost as cold as Siberia. . . .

But what counts most of all is your national trait, your American optimism.

Pavlova with Novikoff in *Don Quixote*, Los Angeles, 1925. *Opposite* Souvenir programme for her last North American tour, 1924–25.

I envy the spirit of your people. I often think how wonderful my country would be if some of your ideas of life prevailed. The greatest thing in America is the tendency of your people to recognize the rights of all to a fair share in the happiness and pleasures created in the land. Yours is true humanity.

Pavlova is nothing if not a feminist and I love her topsy-turvy interpretation of 'equal-rights' when asked about American women. She said:

They are truly wonderful. They are so independent. And they always respond first in the audience. Graceful too. Your men are awkward: they hurry so and rush pell-mell. But the women are the acme of grace. This is the first thing I noticed when I came to America. They are the best ballroom dancers in the world.*

    The modern ballroom dancing: Ah! It is too horrible to mention. . . . Women, keepers of the race, are responsible for the decadence of modern dancing. It is given to them to make the standards, and in this

they have failed. The emancipated woman is largely responsible for all this. She has thrown away something infinitely fine. Man adores her, reveres her, but nothing should do but that she come down to his level. That hideous phrase 'equal rights'! As a consequence man lessens his respect when woman declares herself no longer his superior. The result is what we have today. There are no more little children. The child of eleven or twelve has a fur coat like her mother and, if she so pleases, a diamond ring. At eighteen or nineteen she is sated. Poor child, she grasps eagerly for the thrill of vicious dancing because she has had too much of other pleasures.

These remarks are so revealing of her whole upbringing and outlook which made her almost unable to accept one particular kind of dancing. Pavlova, who would study enthusiastically every kind of national dance, realized only very slowly that 'the modern ballroom dancing', or jazz, was a form of American national dance. In everything else her thinking about dance was often surprisingly 'modern' for the period.

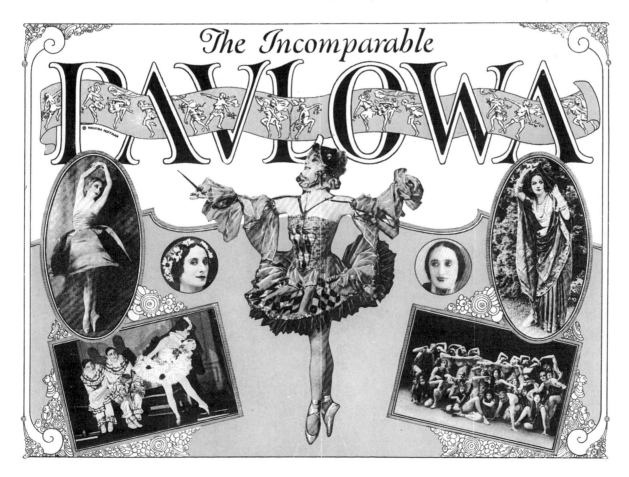

As jazz swept across America and Europe in the 1920s Pavlova was repeatedly asked her opinion of jazz dancing, and I find it quite fascinating to follow the struggle between her worship of beauty and her innate rhythmic response to music.

It was Pavlova herself who said, 'Rhythm is a fundamental fact of life, the key, indeed, to the universe,' and here it was in a form irreconcilable with anything she believed in. At first she hoped it would just go away.

I hate the jazz. I hope the time will soon come when the masses of the people will tire of it, and turn to something more refined.*

I have seen delightfully pretty young ladies dancing the Turkey Trot and the Cake Walk. *C'est horrible! N'est-ce pas?* And I know, because I have tried the Turkey Trot myself, so that I can speak from experience. I am not exaggerating when I say that even today I still sometimes shudder over the experience.*

It is pathetically ludicrous when portly old gentlemen and buxom ladies desperately endeavour to rival their children in acrobatic jazz or that detestable and peculiar Charleston.*

Jazz is terrible. How can people expect to be able to appreciate good music or good anything when they accustom themselves to that? . . .

Now, what does lack of discipline produce in this splendid America? It produces the Shimmie! Ugh!

Time passed but jazz had come to stay – and so had the world's desire to know the great ballerina's opinion of it.

I admit that at its inception I was an uncompromising opponent of the new order in the art of dancing. Gradually, however, I came to hold a modified view.

I have come to the conclusion that to popularize any great institution of art it must be presented in such a form that everybody is interested in it. Thus modern jazz dancing expresses just the spirit of the present age, the abandonment of set forms giving an utter and necessary change from the high tension of everyday life. The strain of our modern existence, caused by the almost unnatural conditions in which we live, would cause us to become either automatons or neurotics unless we were able to find some outlet for emotion.*

Wherever you look there is a new *Palais de Danse*. Everywhere strange music throbs. These are the manifestations of a great discovery by the people. The people have at last found the great joy of the dance. But dancing we have always had, and ballrooms. Then why is it only lately that people have been dancing in their millions?

Because today it is so simple, so easy to learn. After half a dozen lessons the ordinary man or woman can step upon the ballroom floor and dance, if not well, at least well enough to avoid ridicule. Once one would have had to spend years to acquire the minuet, the quadrille, the old waltzes.

In a large American city . . . I went into a vast *Palais de Danse*. The enormous floor was covered with hundreds of couples, and from a raised structure an instructor taught them their dancing by mighty shouts through a megaphone. Thus we can turn out our dancers, like watches and motor-cars, by mass production.

But the most astonishing thing about these new dances is the music. Why do those bizarre melodies arouse emotions of pleasure in multitudes and yet move others to the verge of anger? To be frank, a great deal of it is not music at all. But whatever it may be, it is certainly rhythmic, and you cannot doubt the potent effect of its pulsating harmonies on the dancers.

The endless questions on this subject, about which Pavlova could find very few kind words, continued, and one day brought her to the point where she allowed her impatience to show.

Every interviewer I meet asks me what I think about jazz music, as if he thinks this is a happy topic that nobody else has thought of. I am so tired of the subject that I have begun to dismiss it with the statement that it is all right for those who like it. The music itself is not so bad as what they do with it. The only excuse for dancing is grace and beauty of movement. When these are eliminated in the ugly wriggling movements that some people execute to such music there is no excuse for dancing. However, I don't suppose it will hurt anybody.

Pavlova with Mary Pickford in Hollywood, 1925.

Finally, in 1929, the Liverpool Post *printed what I think is perhaps the most touching of all the interviews in this collection.*

I love the honesty of it – and the contradictions. Here I see a picture of the born dancer carried away in spite of herself, trying to impose her own standards on a form of dancing that in her opinion lacked any standards whatever.

Yes, I have danced jazz – I, who hitherto have looked down scornfully upon modern dances, and condemned them as being ungracious and, indeed, a disgrace to the fine art to which I have devoted the whole of my life. I thought that I should be able to dance jazz in secret. But lo, and behold! It might be thought that a fresh international crisis were threatening. . . .

Because recently in Vienna I joined in the happy throng of dancers, that does not mean to say that my convictions have changed. . . . Yet jazz is not entirely without charm. Some of its forms are considerably more graceful than others . . . if they were only always danced really well. . . . But once and for all, I myself state that this dance appears to me no better than before.

Well then, it will be asked, why did I dance jazz, seeing that I do not approve of jazz as a whole? I am only a woman after all, and as such I am as curious about new things as any other woman, especially where new dances are concerned.

There I was as eager as others to know all about this jazz business, and seeing everybody else joining in the dance, I felt a sudden impulse to be one of them. It was not a beautiful dance, at least, not what I should call beautiful; but it was a dance, for all that. For a brief spell I was dazzled by the flitting, dancing shadows, the changing lights, and the rhythm of the music.

To be candid, I did not 'jazz', in the true meaning of the word. I danced my own dance to jazz music. Being first and foremost a classical dancer, I endeavoured to impart grace to the elementary motions to impress my individuality upon the mechanical uniformity of jazz. I wanted to make a thing of beauty of it, as if I were performing before the public of Paris, Berlin, Rome or London.

The twenties' Pavlova.

Pavlova's excitement always bubbled over whenever she returned to England – which she did frequently in the course of her incessant circlings about the world. Some of her liveliest interviews were those she gave in London on various occasions – such as her arrival in 1925 for a season at Covent Garden.

A dainty vision in black and white, with a bouquet of enormous chrysanthemums in her hands, tripped out of a pullman car at Victoria station on Saturday afternoon. It was Pavlova, smiling happily at the rainy England which she loves.

'No, I'm not the least tired,' she said as I greeted her, 'And my feet are just longing to feel the stage at Covent Garden again.'

I glanced at those wonderful feet neatly shod in low-heeled brown shoes, and the slender ankles encased in woollen stockings.

Perhaps Pavlova read my thoughts. Anyway, she told me that she loved woollen stockings. In fact, she has a penchant for sporting dress, although she herself looks too fairylike to appear on the golf course.⋆

The famous Russian ballerina is one of the most energetic people I know. All day long yesterday she was rehearsing at Covent Garden for the ballet *Giselle*, with which she opens her four weeks' season next Monday. On Saturday, too, within an hour of her arrival, she was on the stage of the Opera House, having changed her velvet travelling cloak and dress for a wisp of gauze. . . .

Since Pavlova left us last autumn she has toured nearly the whole of America. . . . In California she feels very much at home, and, for the first time, she danced for the films in Los Angeles. Mary Pickford was filmed with her, watching a dance.

When I asked her whether she ever had any difficulty about finding a donkey for *Don Quixote* in America, she laughed merrily. 'Ah! the donkey!' she cried. 'He was sometimes very hard to find. In Detroit we searched the whole city in vain, then someone offered us a pony. Fancy Sancho Panza riding on a pony! No, that would be impossible.

'At last we did find a donkey, but he was big, fat and untrained, and instead of him carrying Sancho Panza the stage hands had to carry the donkey on to the stage.'

On her previous London visit she had chattered away about

the rain and given some excellent advice. The current prevalence of bright raincoats only goes to show how much her thoughts raced ahead of the era in which she lived.*

Every time I come to London I notice a difference, sometimes trivial, sometimes important. . . .

This visit it is the change in yourselves that impresses me most. You are waking up at last. In the streets you appear more animated and interested in life; your expression is brighter, your conversation more lively. If you do not take care you will be losing your solid, John Bull reputation one of these days!

But you still do not struggle enough against your old enemy, the climate. When I see you plodding along through the rain in dull, drab mackintoshes, with your noses tucked into your collars, I long to offer you a little advice. It is this: fight the weather with contrasts. . . . You must create an artificial sun to replace the one who has hidden himself. So why not a brighter note in your dress instead of the eternal grey, black, brown or navy?

Yes, I will make an even bolder suggestion. If you *must* wear mackintoshes, why not have them of a brilliant colour? By such means you can snub your old enemy and laugh in his sulky face.

Any celebrity whose fame is dependent on physical skills is likely to attract a morbid interest in how long they can last. One day in London, in 1925, Pavlova read with amazement of her impending retirement, and she reacted immediately by telling reporters:

The suggestion that I am going to retire from the stage is too absurd for words. . . . I shall go on dancing so long as I am able, and I hope that will be for many, many years.

Only a few weeks later an English newspaper recorded:

Flowers thrown from all parts of the house greeted Pavlova on her return to Covent Garden last night. It was a floral welcome without equal in the English theatre for many years.

The great dancer seemed never to have been better – the same ethereal being dancing as if imbued with the spirits of the elements.

With her manager, Edmund Russon, at Victoria station, 1925.

Olivéroff wrote the following beautiful description of Pavlova in the wings preparing for her entrance. This, to me, is like all the ballerinas in the world summed up.

In the theatre Madame invariably crossed herself before each of her entrances. If she went on six times during a performance, then she would cross herself at six different times – I never saw her fail to do so.

How I used to love watching her in the wings, when she was preparing her entrance! There was always a box of resin there for her and she would point first one foot into it, then the other, rubbing the resin into the tips of her ballet shoes so they wouldn't slip on the stage. Often she would stand 'on the point' right in the resin box, and quiver like a butterfly, the better to grind the stuff into the toe of her slipper. She had a real obsession about ballet shoes. They hardly ever suited her. . . . As a rule, she wore a new pair of slippers for every ballet . . . unless, miraculously, she found a pair that pleased her. . . .

When she was through with the resin, she usually bent forward and pressed the palms of her hands to the floor, to limber up her back. Then she pointed her feet, forwards, backwards, and to the sides. And she was forever throwing out her chest and pulling her tunic down at the waist. . . . She would cross herself during any one of these processes – during all of them, indeed, if for any reason she happened to be nervous. She was most apt to cross herself when she was standing on her point in the resin box, and when you saw those graceful knowing hands making the immemorial gesture – not slowly, but fluttering through it with uncanny swiftness – you might have imagined, as I did, that Madame was doing a special little divertissement for the pleasure of Jesus. . . .

Her preparations all made, she would stand there just off-stage, her hand resting on the scenery for support, one leg forward, with the toe pointed at right angles, waiting for her cue to sound from the orchestra. When it sounded, she would fling her arms out stiff behind her, a motion that seemed to put everything in the world but Anna Pavlova behind her, and – zip! – out she would fly.

Opposite Vision scene in *Don Quixote*.

Below Opening night at Covent Garden, 1925. Dancing in *Giselle* with Novikoff.

The real things are what I do on the stage. But how one had to grapple with the hardness of the dream – which, for me, is the daily life, the superintending of production, the re-adjustment of a thousand affairs, the care of my chickens – I mean my girls. They must work, just so. They cannot smoke on the stage or during work. That is the rule. As for smoking elsewhere – this is the modern age: I cannot too closely inquire. They must sleep so much. They must love their art. And they do. They help me so! Each one is a story herself. This one a story of beautiful hands, that one of supremely wonderful feet, another the face, another the expression. All are part of my work. They go with me, back and fro, from the dream to reality, from reality to the dream.

There is nothing one can add to passages like that which are the simple truth of her being. Her company has become her family, for she has no one except her mother, who was able to visit her once for a few summer weeks at Ivy House, then returned to Russia; Victor Dandré is an indispensable part of her life – but that is far from the bond of a true marriage. She knows now that she may never have more – off the stage – and her reality is in the truth with which she invests her every performance.

The Christmas party photograph, taken during a tour of Holland in 1927, tells the whole story, 'wherever I go will be my home'. How touching that picture is, the men in black ties and the girls in their evening 'frocks'. Pavlova always encouraged them to do their hair simply and to wear little jewellery. There you can see all the bitter-sweet gaiety of a 'family' far from its individual families at Christmas. That was the life of the touring theatrical company before air travel became the normal transportation, and also before television changed the entertainment world and dancers started going to parties in blue jeans!

Opposite Christmas in Holland, 1927.

Below Sailing to Australia, 1929. Pierre Vladimiroff is seated in the centre front row, with Pavlova on his left and Ruth French, her English discovery, on his right.

Pavlova took her company to Australia in 1926 and as usual she absorbed every new impression – like a child travelling abroad for the first time.

Sydney people are most artistic . . . so kind, thoughtful and hospitable. A little thing I saw behind the theatre. A man is trying to boil some water to make tea. . . . 'What are you doing,' asked another man, 'trying to boil water in that pot?' Next day he brought him a little electric kettle. I thought it was very kind. But I notice you all want to give.*

Your skies are so blue, and your sun shines so much, and your people, oh! your people, they are so happy, so very happy, always laughing. . . . In my country it is so different, all is sadness, so much unhappiness and starvation, the people do not laugh like you out here, where there seems nothing but joy. . . . [And with a far-away expression, Pavlova clasped her characteristic hands temperamentally, and, shaking her little dark head, she seemed to pull herself together, and smiled rather sadly.] Oh! please forgive me, I must not be sad, and you are all so kind out here, and I appreciate.*

I admire the frocking of the audiences. They are all so beautifully dressed – quite like Paris clothes. But I want to show you what else I like, also [and picking up . . . *Art in Australia*, the gracious dancer turned . . . with a captivating smile]. This, I think, is very good. . . .

You do not have your own opera, no? What a pity. . . . There must be many beautiful voices in this country, where everyone is so happy.

On her second Australian tour in 1929, she was again anxiously looking for signs of artistic development.

[Your] artists must go abroad to become great. They must study in France, Germany, Austria, anywhere but Australia. Why, in Germany, for instance, the whole nation is artistic. Even the working man . . . hears Wagner. His children learn of art always. At eleven they play Chopin. Here . . . many would say, 'Who is this Chopin?' No, you have your gramophones and your dance parties – ugly jazz – and you seem satisfied. And yet you . . . are capable of appreciating . . . more artistic things.

Opposite Sydney, 1926. *Above Gavotte, Sydney, 1929.*

Invitation to the Dance, Sydney, 1929. Pavlova's partner is Pierre Vladimiroff.

Interviewing Madame Pavlova as she was being driven to Perth from Fremantle yesterday was an experience. Into the taxi were crowded the dancer, her husband, several bouquets of flowers, luggage, a representative of the *West Australian*, and three cages of canaries. The ballerina still talked vividly, but now her conversation ran to serious subjects. . . . How was England now? Was the Government settling down to work, and would it be successful in settling some of the great problems there? . . . And Russia? Was there any news? Any – any – 'new' news? Gradually the conversation veered round to Australia. . . .

'This is a beautiful country. . . . But it is . . . a shame that they do not do more for art here. They are funny, these Australians. . . . They seem to be in a – how do you say it? In a – rut. They like art . . . but they take things too much as they come. . . .'

To show the great dancer yet another Australian beauty spot, the taxi was turned into King's Park. She was enraptured with the views of river and city, and expressed surprise at the size of Perth. Three magpies, foraging for lunch, took her fancy. She was sorry to leave the spot, and, as the car drove away, one gained the impression that it was the birds more than the view which would have held her there.

Resuming her conversation, Madame Pavlova expressed her advocacy of Government subsidies to advance art, or, alternatively, private subscriptions. It was not enough, she said, merely to establish art schools, but there should also be, in the theatres, artists who would uplift the community generally. In Russia, when the people struggled against natural calamities, they strove also to protect the arts of their nation. The poorest people, even, felt that Russian art was their heritage and strove to preserve it. Australians could, if they would, become an artistic nation. The secret was enthusiasm.

'Great art needs to be built up on fine ideals,' Madame Pavlova concluded, as the taxi drew up at her hotel, 'and nourished in the right atmosphere. You must always be yourselves. Never pretend. Be good if you can and if you want to. Be bad if you must or if you prefer it. But do not wear a cloak. Be enthusiastic about it. Be earnest, sincere in good or bad. If the Australians lift themselves and drop their – what is it? – Oh, I don't know – "*Laissez*" – the artistic side will come. I'm sure it will.'

As usual, she was far ahead in her thoughts – but right.

It is really amazing to read Pavlova's visions and hopes for the future of dance. One has only to look at ballet in Britain, as an example, to see that everything she suggested has come about in the fifty years since her death.

I think not a little might be done to improve dancing in England by having it taught in your schools. But it should be taught as one of the arts, and not as part of the gymnastic exercises or the sports. Some of your games for girls do not improve deportment. In hockey, for instance, where the girls play in a stooping position, they may easily lose their graceful carriage. . . .

I have found English children who are capable of learning the highest form of the art of dancing. . . . If only more real encouragement were given in England to ballet dancers the day would not be far distant when the English dancer would prove a formidable rival to the Russian.

How can this be done? In the first place, I am strongly of opinion that the English nation ought to endow a National School of Dancing, so that it might take the sadness out of the gait and manner of the English people.★

Look at your girls. As dancers I hold them in the highest esteem. They are hard-working and conscientious, and the only fault I have to find with them is partly due to their English education. From childhood they are taught to control their feelings. Whereas in my art you must dance with abandon and express every emotion.

The English as a nation are athletes and possess the qualities most necessary to the male dancer – strength and agility. If your English athletes excel on the playing field, why not on the stage in the role of *danseur*, which is absolutely indispensable to the successful ballet . . .?★

For a ballet to be really striking the accompaniment must be striking. Feeble music is fatal, and no matter how cleverly the dancers perform . . . there is no effect without a vivid musical accompaniment.★

There are composers in England who are perfectly competent to write good ballet music, and British painters and designers capable of producing scenery and costumes, and teachers able to offer a good technical training.

The misfortune, as far as English dancers are concerned, is that they have in their own country no opera or other theatre in which they can expound the serious and classical side of dancing.★

You will never have great dancing nor great opera in your country till it is sufficiently helped and protected. It requires to be adequately financed.

But most extraordinary of all are her ideas about a ballet without music. This may not seem strange to us until we realize that the following passage is taken from an interview she gave in America in 1915!

It has been my dream to perfect the dancing of myself and my company to the extent that music should become only an accentuation instead of the dominating factor. I have no doubt that this is possible, for whenever I think of new dances these dances suggest tonalities to me. I am not a composer, so I could not express in black dots the music that is running through my brain, but I can hear it, and so could the audience, provided the plastic art of the dancers could be brought to perfection.

No ideal ballet music has ever been written. The dancer has been considered only as an interpreter and has necessarily been limited in her efforts to the expression of the composer's ideas; but just as a colour may and does suggest a musical tonality, so should a dance create in the brain a musical picture. . . . When we speak of music creating certain pictures in the minds of the hearers we state an uncontrovertible fact, and it is logical to suppose that dancing should call forth a melody in the brain of those who witness it, provided, in both cases, that the respective art has reached a high mark.

No doubt should I or somebody else decide upon presenting a ballet without the musical accompaniment the idea would be greeted with derision. But it would be an interesting experiment, making every man and woman his or her own composer, and if the dancers possessed the necessary talent it would be well worth while. I am planning to try the experiment of a ballet without music some day. Of course it would have to be before an invited audience, for the innovation would be too radical to attract the masses; besides I do not believe anybody would be willing to pay for a performance of that kind.

In the garden at Ivy House, 1930.

The timeless portrait.

How ironical that Pavlova, who in 1915 could foresee ballets without music, struck a period in time when the quirks of fashion ruled that she was outmoded. Critics found the music of Giselle *'beyond the pale' but one hears few complaints these days about far flimsier stuff – and the Petipa ballets she loved are performed far more frequently than most of the Diaghilev repertoire. It is not that Diaghilev's genius is in doubt, nor his vital influence diminished, but simply that with the passing of time taste has – for the moment – swung back to accepting even the lesser works of the nineteenth century and pre-Diaghilev era. How interesting that in 1910 Pavlova had said, 'Whatever direction the ballet reformers take, Petipa's innovations will remain with us for ever.'*

In 1929 she gave an interview at the Golders Green Hippodrome – only a few hundred yards down the road from her home, Ivy House.

She holds her head back, her shoulders very straight; she sits poised like a swan.

She sits very still.

Our questions come to her and she receives them like some weary, all-wise being. She is still calm, only her dark eyes move restlessly from speaker to speaker. They are two separate beings in that white, unlined face.

Then she smiles, and the fires snap and flicker in those living dark lakes.

We see again the coquette, the ultra-feminine, capricious, lovable woman as she parries a question, breaking into quick Russian or turning to one of the old friends who, like some faithful bodyguard of a fallen monarchy, stand behind her chair as though to protect a queen from the eager onslaught of a new generation of questioning, querying minds.

'Do you think that the ballet should be modernized, made to grow and change with the times?'

She spreads the fingers of one hand in a quick, fluttering, deprecating movement.

'The ballet is in itself classical: the dance cannot change and remain so perfect . . . the décor, the music, even the costume; but the dance – no. . . .'

She sighed: this little figure in black and white. Below her throat is a mark – some say of a bullet-shot. She is one of the strange, romantic figures of life; not only a Swan, perhaps, but rather the Seagull as Tchekov saw it, white and beautiful and tragic.

'What of the ballet in Russia today? Ah, I do not know; it is long since I have been in Russia; it has kept, so I hear, the classical traditions of the old days . . . but I do not know the Russia of today.'

She broke off: this beautiful, proud thing, she who had been the darling of an Imperial court, feted by princes and grand-dukes in those old, almost mythical days.

There seemed a touch of autumn, of sadness in those unfathomable dark eyes. The old order. . . .

There has never been a dancer such as the lovely Russian Swan.

Pavlova has not changed, not grown older one day. Her art is identical: flawless, exquisite, infinitely polished.

But the world has gone on. She is beautiful, but already even in the flesh mythical.

What of Pavlova, the woman? . . . Behind that personality of the Perfect Dancer is a warmly human nature. She is loved, feared and adored by the members of her company. There is nothing she would hold back from her art and she demands something of the same standard from those who dance with her.

'We have had a wonderful tour, but even in the Red Sea, on our return from Australia, we had to practise,' said Miss Ruth French, who is Pavlova's star discovery – and English. . . .

'Do you live only for your art, Madame?' I ventured.

'Oh, yes . . . but then my life has other things in it,' she flashed. 'For instance, my birds, my famous birds of which I am so fond, have had to be left behind on this trip. Nevertheless, I have brought some other strange pets to London with me. Especially I do love my dog, Lebbo. . . . He is such a dear. . . .

'Our plans? We intend to visit Spain, and afterwards we will go for one performance to Paris. . . . Then, I do not know.'

There is no ageing for this woman: she seems tireless – taut – vibrant with energy, and pathos lurks in the passing not of Pavlova, the immortal, but of time itself, which has seen her and gone on to other things.

It is not because Pavlova is Pavlova, but because the circumstance and order of life are different, have changed irrevocably, that Anna Pavlova, the lovely Swan of all the dreams in the world, dances, not at Covent Garden, but at Golders Green.

My home, where is it? It is everywhere. Everywhere my audiences welcome me.★

I should, of course, say that what I really long for in my heart of hearts is a quiet secluded corner far from the crowd, a home, immovable and dependable, and domesticity. But that would not be true.

I feel as contented and domestic in a railroad train or in my stateroom on an ocean liner as I do anywhere. I have come to regard the wide world, and not any particular place, as my home. And if I could not see many places and people, and discover their souls, I would feel that I was leading an unprofitable existence. . . .

Perhaps my pleasure in wandering and my longing to encounter the real, inner things in the lives of people would have led me nowhere if I had not been able to preserve something permanent, enduring, and beautiful from my discoveries, in my art. For the things I put on the stage with my company, my painters, musicians, choreographers and so forth are points of fulfilment and, so to speak, repose, in my life. Indeed, they are so much the actualities for me, that often they alone are real, and all else that occurs a mirage, misleading, non-existent.★

I am a sower, I am but scattering the seeds. If I should live to see the harvest of my work how happy I should be. But that is asking too much. I must be content with my today.

Pavlova is now nearing fifty, with her childhood ambitions fulfilled beyond imagination.

She is a world citizen, but an exile for the rest of her life – which will be much shorter than anyone could guess in 1930 – and it is we who enjoy the harvest of her work. How one wishes she could see the dance world as it is today.

Opposite In her favourite corner of the garden at Ivy House in September 1930, on the eve of her last provincial tour of England.

Below At Leicester Station, 4 December 1930.

To the end Pavlova maintained an amazing schedule of performances with her company – which she knew would cease to exist if she did not dance. In any case she must dance; she never really had, or wished to have, any alternative. It was not from mere ambition, which is a word I associate rather more with the desire for personal acclaim and riches. I believe that Pavlova's compulsion to give of herself to help others, her idealism and her need to express herself through movement, gradually overwhelmed all other dreams, hopes and ambitions she may have had in her youth. She said it herself in a very simple way.

I think that a real artist should irrevocably and completely dedicate herself to art. . . . I have realized that true art gives joy not only to the artist but also to the people, suspending them for a moment from life's sorrows. In this I see the great significance of art, and the awareness of this became the aim of my life. . . .

But what is success? I do not find it in the applause of the theatre, but in the realization of one's ideal. Once when I was a child I used to think that success meant happiness. I was wrong. Happiness is a butterfly, which appears briefly for a moment and then flies away.

Death came surreptitiously. The account of Pavlova's last few days was written by Valerian Svetlov, who lived in Paris with Vera Trefilova, Pavlova's close friend since they were together in the Imperial School.

Christmas 1930 had been spent in Cannes and, as usual, Pavlova was anxious to get back into practice before starting a new tour.

Returning from Cannes, where she had been resting for three weeks after a tiring tour around England, Pavlova was involved in a train accident. . . . She got out of her warm coach, half-dressed, into the cold night air. I do not know if she was already ill when she arrived in Paris – it was difficult to tell because of her dislike of admitting to illness and because of her truly iron will. I saw her the next day in Trefilova's studio, where she went . . . to practise 'to make up for the time lost in Cannes', for Pavlova always consi-

dered time without work to be lost time. She was due to go to The Hague four days later, from where she was to begin her long tour around Holland, Belgium, Germany, Poland and the Baltic states.

'We people who work are not allowed to be ill,' she told me. 'I must pull myself together.' When Trefilova asked her how she felt, she pointed to her chest and put her finger to her lips, as if she meant that no one was to know about this. She asked for the studio to be heated before changing into her dance clothes, and put her underclothing on the radiators to warm it – something she had never done before. It is only now that all this strikes me as being the faint indication of an unsatisfactory state of health.

As usual, she practised enthusiastically with her partner, Pierre Vladimiroff. She was annoyed because she had put on two kilos during her holiday, and now she had to lose them again before going to The Hague. She was in a lively mood and recalled with Trefilova their days at the Maryinsky, for they were made ballerinas on the same evening. As she bade Trefilova farewell on the night before her departure, she said in a sad voice, 'We haven't yet had a rest together, Verochka. . . . Now there's not much . . .' She did not finish the sentence. . . .

When she arrived at The Hague towards evening she was given a grand welcome at the station, with flowers, speeches and ovations. She had the courage to listen to all this with a smile upon her lips. But once she reached her hotel she went to bed immediately with a temperature of 39.9°. The inflammation of the lungs grew progressively worse and . . . her back was pierced to drain away the fluid. . . . A general poisoning of the blood set in several hours before she died. Anna Pavlova sank into a drowsy state and departed into eternity. . . .

Thus suddenly ended with lightning speed the brief life of this great artist, the eternal wanderer, on one of the stages of her last journey. . . .

She died having devoted her whole being to art. She did not betray it once. . . .

When she so touchingly said, a few days before her death, that she had not yet had time to rest, she was right. It was a cry from a soul which gave way to a moment's weariness.

The Dying Swan.

The funeral service for Anna Pavlova, whose remains were cremated afterwards at Golders Green, was held yesterday [29 January 1931] in the Russian Church in Buckingham Palace Road. God's glorification proceeded according to a rich and ancient ritual of Russia, whose essence is the application to religion of those things of the earth in which humanity delights. Gold and jewels are precious to man: bring them, then, to churches, and use them in the adornment of pictures and images.

Flowers are lovely: offer them in profusion to their Creator. Incense is pleasurable: let it smell sweetly to heaven. Pavlova sought beauty in dancing, and beauty is, surely, divine. I see no reason why people should not dance before God. The worship of old Russia is so human that it seems almost voluptuous to one of a colder faith. The dead dancer, who had infused us with something of her ecstasy, lay in the middle of the church. Her coffin was draped with the Russian flag.

Immortal Pavlova

It was banked with countless wreaths and flowers. Six candles, three at each side, burned beside it. Candles lined the altar screen. Candles, held by men, women and children, flickered among the congregation. Candlelight, mingled with sunlight, glowed in the gold robes of the clergy who stood at the head of the coffin. The whole place swam in incense and music. The choir was unseen. A man chanted superbly in a deep, sonorous voice. The choir replied urgently, rhythmically.

Their voices were wave upon wave of exquisite sound. One of the clergy drenched the coffin with incense, and the clash of the chains of his censer penetrated the singing. The priest was bearded, remote, and splendid in his gold vestments. The singing rose again, and in its tide, the clergy passed through the altar screen, closing its doors behind them and drawing a veil across its doors. Old Russia had reclaimed Pavlova in England, and committed her soul to God.

Somewhere in every one of us, no matter how deep it may be hidden,
is a latent germ of beauty. . . . We dance because this germ of beauty
demands such expression, and the more we give it outlet the more
we encourage our own instinct for graceful forms. It is by the steady elimination
of everything which is ugly – thoughts and words no less than tangible objects –
and by the substitution of things of true and lasting beauty that
the whole progress of humanity proceeds.

1881
Born in St Petersburg, 31 January,★ daughter of Matvey Pavlovich Pavlov and Liubov Feodorovna Pavlova.

1891
Admitted to the Imperial Ballet School.

1899
Graduation. Joins the Imperial Ballet.

1904
Guest appearances in Moscow and Warsaw.

1905
Promoted to Principal Dancer.

1908
Guest appearances in Riga. Tour of Scandinavia, Germany and Czechoslovakia.

1909
Guest appearances in Germany, Czechoslovakia and Austria. Appears with Diaghilev company in Paris. Makes London debut at private party; meets King Edward.

1910
New York debut, Metropolitan Opera House. First season at Palace Theatre, London. Returns to St Petersburg and requests two-year leave of absence. Begins first North American tour, with Mikhail Mordkin and small group of soloists.

1911
Second season at Palace Theatre, London. Appears with Diaghilev company at Royal Opera House, London. First English provincial tour.

1912
Moves into Ivy House, London. Third season at Palace Theatre. Begins tour of Germany.

1913
Last performance at Maryinsky. Fourth season at Palace Theatre. Forms her own company on a permanent basis. Begins six-month North American tour.

1914
Guest appearances in Germany, Austria, Czechoslovakia and Hungary. Last performance in Russia. Further appearances in Germany. Begins six-month North American tour.

1915
First visit to Cuba. Makes feature film 'The Dumb Girl of Portici'. Forms joint opera-ballet company with which she tours the U.S. for nine months.

1916
Long engagement at the New York Hippodrome, in 'The Big Show'.

1917–19
Tour of Latin America. Guest appearances in Spain and France.

1920
Returns to London; seasons at Drury Lane and Prince's theatres. Begins six-month North American tour.

1921
Guest appearances in Paris. Season at Queen's Hall, London. Begins six-month North American tour.

1922
First tour of the East, starting in Japan.

1923
Continues tour of the East, ending in Egypt. Guest appearances in Paris. First season at Royal Opera House, London. Begins six-month North American tour.

1924
Guest appearances in Paris. Second season at Royal Opera House, London. Begins (last) six-month North American tour.

1925
Guest appearances in Paris. Tour of Germany. Third season at Royal Opera House, London. Sails for South Africa.

1926
Tour of South Africa, Australia and New Zealand. Begins six-month European tour.

1927
Continues European tour. Last season at Royal Opera House, London. Begins six-month European tour.

1928
Second tour of Latin America. Begins second tour of the East in Egypt.

1929
Continues tour of the East; India, Singapore, Java. Second tour of Australia. English provincial tour.

1930
Extended tour of Europe, ending in Paris. Last English provincial tour. Christmas and New Year in Cannes.

1931
12 January Arrives in Paris from Cannes. 17 January Leaves Paris for The Hague. 23 January Dies in the Hôtel des Indes, The Hague.

★ Russian dates throughout this book are given in the Old Style. For corresponding dates in the Western calendar, add twelve days in the nineteenth century, and thirteen in the twentieth.

Ballets Illustrated

Page	Ballet	Choreographer	Composer
frontispiece	*Christmas*	Pavlova, Clustine, Volinine	Tchaikovsky
8 & 147	*The Dying Swan*	Fokine	Saint-Saëns
12	*Dragonfly*	Pavlova	Kreisler
24	*The Seasons*	Petipa	Glazunov
25	*The Awakening of Flora*	Petipa, Ivanov	Drigo
26–7, 52 & 133	*Giselle*	Coralli, Perrot/Petipa	Adam
33	*La Fille Mal Gardée*	Dauberval/Petipa, Ivanov	Hertel
35	*Swan Lake*	Petipa, Ivanov	Tchaikovsky
36	Chopin *valse*	Fokine	Chopin
37	*La Nuit*	N. Legat	Rubinstein
38–39	*Russian Dance*	Mordkin	Tchaikovsky/Alabiev
42	*Coppélia*	Saint-Léon/Saracco	Delibes
46–7 & 118	*Valse Caprice*	N. Legat	Rubinstein
51	*Legend of Aziade*	Mordkin	Rimsky-Korsakov et al.
60–61	*Le Pavillon d' Armide*	Fokine	N. Tcherepnin
73	*Autumn Leaves*	Pavlova	Chopin
74	*La Bayadère*	Petipa	Minkus
77	*Bacchanale*	Mordkin	Glazunov
82, 100, 138–9	*Invitation to the Dance*	Zajlich	Weber
82	*The Magic Flute*	Ivanov/Pavlova, Cecchetti	Drigo
86	*The Fairy Doll*	N. & S. Legat/Clustine	Bayer, Rubinstein et al.
90	*Carmen*	Clustine	Bizet
92	*The Sleeping Beauty*	Petipa/Clustine	Tchaikovsky
98 & 108	*Amarilla*	Zajlich	Glazunov et al.
99 & 137	*Gavotte*	Clustine	Lincke
112	*Ajanta Frescoes*	Clustine	A. Tcherepnin
115	*Krishna and Radha*	Shankar	Banerji
115	*Hindu Wedding*	Shankar	Banerji
122	*The Butterfly*	Pavlova	Minkus
124 & 134	*Don Quixote*	Gorsky/Novikoff	Minkus/Drigo

Photographic Acknowledgments

Leningrad State Theatre Museum: pages 19, 30, 32 (below), 60, 61
The Museum of London: pages 27 (below), 46, 47, 52, 87, 88, 89, 99, 112, 115 (below), 131, 144, 145
The New York Public Library, Picture Collection: page 37
The Royal Ballet School: pages 14, 16
The Times (London): page 133
University of Washington Libraries, Seattle, Special Collections Division: page 51 (below)

All other photographs are from the collaborators' collections.

Numbers refer to paragraphs of quoted text.
Where no number is given, only one source is applicable.

Page 9
The Frederick Ashton article first appeared in the Catalogue to 'Pavlova: An Exhibition on her Life and Work', presented by the Globe Playhouse, London, 26 January to 5 February 1965.

Page 11
The quotation in Margot Fonteyn's Introduction is from the *Buenos Aires Herald*, 10 August 1917.

Page 13
Manchester Evening News, 30 October 1925.

Page 15
Anna Pavlova, 'Reflections', in *The Ladies' Home Journal* (Philadelphia), September 1924.

Page 17
1 Unidentified press cutting, entitled 'Ballet of the Classic Kind'.
2–4 Anna Pavlova, 'Pages of My Life', in *Lectures pour Tous*, Paris, 1 June 1913. Translated by Sebastien Voirol.
5 *The Sun* (Indianapolis), 27 October 1910; quoted in *Dance Magazine* (New York), January 1956.
6 & 7 'Pages of My Life'.
8 *The Sun* (Indianapolis).

Page 18
The Sun (Indianapolis), 27 October 1910.

Pages 20 & 21
1 *Vanity Fair* (London), 16 July 1914.
2 & 3 'Ballet of the Classic Kind'.
4 & 5 *Pall Mall Gazette* (London), 25 April 1910.
6 *Vanity Fair* (New York), February 1915.
7 & 8 *Pall Mall Gazette*.
9 *Vanity Fair* (New York).
10 'Ballet of the Classic Kind'.
11–13 'Reflections'.
14–16 *Vanity Fair* (London).
17 & 18 *Pall Mall Gazette*.
19 *Leeds Mercury*, 4 March 1912.

Page 23
'Reflections'.

Page 25
Petersburgskaya gazeta, 12 November 1909.

Page 27
Tamara Karsavina, in *Slavonic Review*, London, March 1931.

Page 29
1 & 2 Unidentified cutting, dated 1910, from Valerian Svetlov's press book.
3 *Petersburgskaya gazeta*, 12 November 1909.
4 *The Sun* (Indianapolis), 27 October 1910.

Pages 30 & 31
Svetlov press book.

Page 33
1–3 'Reflections'.
4 *The Sun* (New York), 12 November 1916.

Page 34
1–3 *Dance Magazine* (New York), May 1928.
4ff. *Vanity Fair* (London), 16 July 1914.

Page 36
1 & 2 *Daily Express* (London), 11 September 1927.
3–5 *Vanity Fair* (London), 16 July 1914.
6 & 7 *Daily Mail* (London), 21 July 1909.

Page 38
1 *Daily Mail* (London), 21 July 1909.
2 *Vanity Fair* (London), 16 July 1914.
3 & 4 *Daily Mail*.
5 *Daily Express* (London), 11 September 1927.
6 *Dance Magazine* (New York), June 1928.

Page 41
1–3 *Petersburgskaya gazeta*, 12 November 1909.
4ff. *Petersburgskaya gazeta*, 27 August 1909.

Page 43
Musical America (New York), 5 March 1910.

Page 45
New York Times, 6 March 1910.

Page 46
1 *Tatler* (London), 27 April 1910.
2 ff. *Daily Express* (London), 11 September 1927.

Page 49
Letter from Pavlova to M. Gorshkova, dated 8 August 1910.

Page 53
The Sun (Indianapolis), 27 October 1910.

Page 55
1 *The Sun* (Indianapolis), 27 October 1910.
2 *Pall Mall Gazette* (London), 25 April 1910.
3ff. *The Sun* (Indianapolis).

Page 56
Victor Dandré, *Anna Pavlova in Art and Life* (London: Cassell, 1932).

Page 59
Tatler (London), 2 August 1911.

Page 61
1 *Daily Express* (London), 11 September 1927.
2 *Times Weekly* (London), 20 September 1925.
3 *Leeds Mercury*, 4 March 1912.

Page 62
1 & 2 *Leeds Mercury*, 4 March 1912.
3 *Daily Mail* (London), 2 November 1911.

Page 64
Daily Mail (London), 2 November 1911.

Page 67
1 *Dance Magazine* (New York), June 1928.
2 Quoted in Keith Money, *Anna Pavlova* (New York: Alfred A. Knopf, 1982).
3 & 4 *Vanity Fair* (London), 16 July 1914.
5 *Pall Mall Gazette* (London), 5 August 1913.

Pages 68 & 69
Home Chat (London), 1 November 1924.

Page 70
Dancing World (New York), 10 January 1914.

Page 73
1 *The Sun* (Indianapolis), 27 October 1910.
2 Valerian Svetlov, 'The Soul of Anna Pavlova'. Unidentified press cutting, dated January 1931, Svetlov press book.
3ff. Sydney Dark, 'The Dancer Who Thinks', in *The Strand Magazine*, London, October 1924.

Page 74
Birzhevye vedomosti (St Petersburg), 10 January 1913.

Page 76
1 *Health and Strength* (London), 16 October 1926.
2–6 Montage of unidentified press cuttings relating to Pavlova's 1913 season at the Palace Theatre, London.
7ff. Frederick Ashton, as told to Richard Buckle. Unidentified press cutting.

Page 79
The Sun (New York), 8 June 1913.

Page 82
1 *Daily News* (London), 22 November 1925.
2ff. *Dance Magazine* (New York), May 1928.

Page 85
Quoted in Keith Money, *Anna Pavlova* (New York: Alfred A. Knopf, 1982).

Page 87
Unidentified press cutting, Dandré press file.

Page 88
Dandré.

Page 90
1 *Los Angeles Times*, 7 January 1916.
2 *Boston Transcript*, 29 October 1915.
3 *Kansas City Post*, 9 April 1916.
4 & 5 *Boston Herald*, 17 December 1915.

Page 93
Sol Hurok, in collaboration with Ruth Goode, *Impresario* (London: Macdonald, 1947).

Page 94
1 'Reflections'.
2ff. *San Francisco Chronicle*, 3 December 1924.

Page 96
1 *New York Times*, 7 January 1917.
2–4 *Dancing World* (New York), August/September 1923.
5ff. *The Dance* (New York), July 1927.

Page 98
1 & 2 *Daily Express* (London), 21 October 1925.
3–5 *Daily News* (London), 22 November 1925.
6ff. Theodore Stier, *With Pavlova Round the World* (London: Hurst & Blackett, 1929).

Page 101
1 *Buenos Aires Herald*, 10 August 1917.
2 André Olivéroff, *Flight of the Swan: A Memory of Anna Pavlova* (New York: Dutton, 1932).
3ff. *Buenos Aires Herald*.

Page 102
Observer (London), 12 June 1921.

Page 105
Dance Magazine (New York), June 1928.

Page 106
1 & 2 *Daily News* (London), 22 November 1925.
3 *The Dance* (New York), July 1927.
4 *Dancing Times* (London), October 1923.
5 Harcourt Algeranoff, *My Years With Pavlova* (London: Heinemann, 1957).

Page 109
Ryunosuke Akutagawa, 'Russian Ballet at the Imperial Theatre', in *The New Stage Art (Shin-Engei Magazine)*, Tokyo, October 1922. Translated by Kenji Usui.

Page 110
1–3 Stier.
4ff. *Times of India* (Bombay), 24 December 1928.

Page 113
1–3 Stier.
4ff. *Boston Sunday Post*, 4 November 1923.

Page 114
1–8 *Statesman* (Calcutta), 6 January 1929.
9 *Dance Magazine* (New York), July 1928.
10ff. *Boston Sunday Post*, 4 November 1923.

Page 116
Boston Sunday Post, 4 November 1923.

Page 119
1 *The Sun* (Indianapolis), 27 October 1910.
2 & 3 *Daily Express* (London), 21 October 1925.

Page 120
1 & 2 *Dance Magazine* (New York), July 1928.
3 *The Sun* (New York), 7 January 1917.
4–6 *Dance Magazine*.
7 *Sioux Daily Tribune*, 1 January 1921.
8 *New York Times*, 7 January 1917.
9 *San Francisco Chronicle*, 14 January 1924.
10 *San Francisco Examiner*, 4 February 1921.

Page 123
1–3 *Los Angeles Examiner*, 29 July 1916.
4 *San Francisco Examiner*, 4 February 1921.
5–10 *Los Angeles Examiner*, 8 February 1921.
11–13 *The Sun* (Indianapolis), 27 October 1910.

Page 125
1 *Butte Daily Post*, 11 January 1921.
2 *The Sun* (Indianapolis), 27 October 1910.
3 *San Francisco Examiner*, 4 February 1921.

Page 126
1 *Toronto Star Weekly*, 20 November 1920.
2 *The Strand Magazine* (London), October 1913.
3 *Health and Strength* (London), 16 October 1926.
4 & 5 *Denver Post*, 26 February 1921.
6 & 7 *Daily Chronicle* (London), 13 October 1925.
8–11 *Daily Mail* (London), 2 October 1925.
12 *The Dance* (New York), July 1927.

Source References

Page 128
Liverpool Post, 1 August 1929.

Page 130
1–4 *Daily Express* (London), 21 September 1925.
5–8 *Daily Graphic* (London), 24 September 1925.
9–12 *Daily Mail* (London), 24 October 1924.
13 *Morning Post* (London), 26 September 1925.
14 & 15 *Manchester Dispatch*, 29 September 1925.

Page 133
Olivéroff

Page 135
Boston Sunday Post, 4 November 1923.

Page 136
1 *Daily Telegraph* (Sydney), 22 April 1926.

2 *Sydney Morning Herald*, 22 April 1926.
3 & 4 *Daily Telegraph*.
5 *West Australian* (Perth), 10 July 1929.

Page 139
West Australian (Perth), 10 July 1929.

Page 140
1–3 *The Strand Magazine* (London), October 1913.
4 & 5 *Daily Herald* (London), 25 September 1930.
6 *The Sun* (New York), 12 November 1916.
7 & 8 *Daily Herald*.
9 *Edinburgh Evening News*, 3 November 1925.
10ff. *Boston Transcript*, 29 October 1915.

Page 143
J. M. Burns, 'The Return of Anna Pavlova', in *Queen*, London, 11 December 1929.

Page 145
1 Pavlova Souvenir Programme, Sydney, 1926.
2–4 *Boston Sunday Post*, 4 November 1923.
5 *San Francisco Examiner*, 4 February 1921.

Page 146
1 & 2 Anna Pavlova, 'Pages of My Life'; quoted in Valerian Svetlov, 'The Soul of Anna Pavlova'.
3ff. 'The Soul of Anna Pavlova'.

Pages 148 & 149
Daily Express (London), 30 January 1931.

Page 150
Daily Graphic (London), 26 October 1925.

Index

Page numbers in *italic* type refer to the illustrations.

Ajanta Frescoes, 113, 114; *113*
Akutagawa, Ryunosuke, 109
Alexander III, Tsar of Russia, 23, 45
Alexandra, Queen of England, 36, 38
Alexandria, *116*
Algeranoff, Harcourt, 106, 115
Allegri, Orest, 115
Amarilla, 106, 109; *98, 109*
American Red Cross, *86*
Argentina, 101
Art in Australia, 136
Ashton, Sir Frederick, 9
Astruc, Gabriel, 74
Atwell, Ben, 53, 55
Auber, Daniel-François-Esprit, 87
Australia, 9, 96, 136, 139; *135, 137*
Austria, 34, 136
Autumn Leaves, 73, 106; *73*
The Awakening of Flora, 25; *25*

Bacchanale, 77
Bakst, Léon, 90, 93; *90*
Balanchine, George, 23
Ballet Russe, 61
Baltic states, 146
La Bayadère, 25, 29; *74*
Belgium, 146
Bergé, Marcel, *80*
Berlin, 41, 43, 61, 82, 87, 128; *83*
Bombay, 114; *110*
Boni, Mr, 61
Boston Grand Opera Company, 87, 90
Brazil, 99
Brunswick, 82
Buddha, 113
Buenos Aires, 61, 101
The Butterfly, 59, 123; *122*

Cairo, *116*
Calcutta, 61, 114
California, 120, 130
Cannes, 146
Carmen, *90*
Cecchetti, Enrico, 29, 30, 56; *29*
Centanini G.P., 51
Chicago Opera, 123
China, 110

Chopin, Frédéric, 36, 59, 96, 106, 136
Chopin *valse*, 36, 59; *36*
Chopiniana, 106, 109
Christmas, frontispiece
Clustine, Ivan, *93*
The Constant Love, 61
Coppélia, 41, 43; *42*
Le Corsaire, 29
Costa Rica, 101
Covent Garden, 59, 61, 130, 143; *103, 133*
Cuba, 96, 101; *96*

Dandré, Victor, 11, 56, 88, 94, 135; *94*
Daughter of the Pharaoh, 23
Degas, Edgar, 102
Denmark, 41
Detroit, 130
Diaghilev, Serge, 34, 41, 43, 59, 61, 90, 143
Don Quixote, 29, 130; *124, 133*
Doughty, John Carr, 11
Dragonfly, *12*
The Dumb Girl of Portici (film), 87–8, 90; *87, 88*
Duncan, Isadora, 102
The Dying Swan, 61, 70, 73, 109; *8, 70, 146*

Edward VII, King of England, 36, 38
Egypt, 110; *116*
Empress of Canada (ship), *104*
England, 36–8, 41, 46, 59–69, 74–9, 87, 130, 140, 146

The Fairy Doll, 106; *86*
La Fille Mal Gardée, *32–3*
Finlandia (ship), *121*
First World War, 82–7, 90, 96, 101, 102
Fokine, Michel, 25, 29
Foster, Mr, 61
France, 34, 74, 123, 136, 146
Fremantle, 139
French, Ruth, 143; *135*
Fresno, 120

Galli, Rosina, 56
Gavotte, *98, 137*
Gerdt, Pavel, 25, 29, 30
Germany, 34, 41, 82, 87, 136, 146

Giraud, 59
Giselle, 9, 25, 27, 29, 41, 43, 51, 73, 130, 143; *27, 53, 133*
Golders Green, 148
Golders Green Hippodrome, 143
Guayaquil, 101

The Hague, 146
Hankin, St John, 61
Havana, 96, 101; *96*
Helpmann, Sir Robert, 9
Hindu Wedding, 115
Hindus, 114
Holland, 135, 146; *135*
Hollywood, 87–8; *127*
Home Chat, 68–9
The Humpbacked Horse, 74
Hurok, Sol, 93, 94

Imperial Ballet School, St Petersburg, 15, 20–1, 23, 33, 93, 94, 146; *15, 18, 20, 21*
Imperial Theatre, St Petersburg, 23, 43, 79
Imperial Theatre, Tokyo, 106; *106*
India, 110–14; *110*
Indiana, 53
Indianapolis Sun, 53
Invitation to the Dance, 82, 100, 139
Italy, 29, 56, 96, 123
Ivy House, 67–9, 79, 135, 143; *67–9, 79, 110, 141, 145*

Japan, 105, 106, 109–10, 113, 114; *105, 106*
Johansson, Christian, 25, 29

Kahn family, 123
Karsavina, Tamara, 25, 27, 34
Kchessinskaya, Matilda, 25, 30
Kikugoro, *106*
Krishna and Radha, 115

Lake, Molly, 106
Lappa, V. P., 25
Latin America, 96–100
Lazzarini, John, 11
Lazzarini, Roberta, 11
Leeds, 62
Leeds Mercury, 61, 62
Legat, Nicolas, *34*

Legend of Aziade, 51; *51*
Legnani, Pierina, 25, 27
Leicester, *145*
Lima, 9, 101; *100*
Liszt, Franz, 96
Liverpool Post, 128
Londesborough, Lady, 36
London, 36–8, 41, 43, 46, 59–69, 74–9, 128, 130; *131, 133*
Los Angeles, 56, 130; *124*
Los Angeles Examiner, 123
Los Angeles Times, 90
Lounatcharsky, 102

The Magic Flute, 25; *83*
Manchester, 13
Manchester Evening News, 13
Marie, Empress, 36
Maryinsky Theatre, St Petersburg, 17, 20, 23, 25, 27, 33, 41, 49, 74, 79, 146; *17*
Metropolitan Opera House, New York, 41, 43, 123
Mexico, 98
Mexico City, 98; *98*
Milan, 29, 41, 56
Monte Carlo, 61
Mordkin, Michel, 36, 38, 46, 51, 53, 59, 76; *46, 51, 58*
Moscow, 102

Nashville, 120
National Opera, Havana, 96
Nautch dancers, 113
The New Stage Art, 109
New York, 41, 43–6, 49, 61, 87
New York Hippodrome, 90, 93, 96; *90*
New York Sun, 79
New York Times, 45
Nicholas II, Tsar of Russia, 79
Nicolini, Romeo, 56
Nijinsky, Vaslav, 25, 34, 61; *60*
Nikisch, Arthur, 45
Novikoff, Laurent, 59, 76; *77, 83, 113, 124, 133*
La Nuit, 37

The Observer, 102
Odell, Frank, 53, 55

Olivéroff, André, 11, 101, 133
Oriental Impressions, 114; *115*
Oscar, King of Sweden, 34

Palace Theatre, London, 41, 46, 59, 76
Panama, 101
Papillons, see The Butterfly
Paquita, 29
Paris, 34, 36, 41, 43, 61, 64, 74, 102, 123, 128, 146
Le Pavillon d'Armide, 60
Pavlova, Liubov (Pavlova's mother), 15, 17, 18, 20, 135; *17*
Pavlova Imperial Ballet Russe, 90
Pavlova Society, 11
Pavlovsk, *80*
Persia, 113
Perth, 139
Petipa, Marius, 15, 25, 143
Pickford, Mary, 130; *127*
Plate, River, 101
Pleshcheyev, Alexander, 23

Poland, 146
Preobrajenskaya, Olga, 25, 30

Rabinoff, Max, 51
Riga, 33
Rio de Janeiro, 61
Rome, 123, 128
La Rose Qui Meurt, 59
Rubinstein, Anton, 36, 59
Russia, 15–27, 33, 73–4, 79, 123, 135, 139, 143, 148
Russian Church, Buckingham Palace Road, 148–9; *148–9*
Russian dance, 38, 59; *38*
Russon, Edmund, *131*

St Petersburg, 17, 18, 73, 74, 79; *15, 17*
Saint-Saëns, Camille, 96
Santiago, 101
Scandinavia, 34
The Seasons, 25
Selfridge's, London, 61, 64
Serov, Valentin (drawing), *4*
Shanghai, 110

Shaw, George Bernard, 106
Sioux City, 61
The Sleeping Beauty, 17, 29, 41, 90, 93; *93*
Smallens, Alexander, *93*
Sokolova, E. P., 25, 29, 41
Sotheby's, London, 11
South America, 96, 101
Spain, 67, 96
Statesman, 114
Stier, Theodore, 11, 98, 110, 113; *93*
Stockholm, 34
Stuart, Muriel, 66
Svetlov, Valerian, 73, 146; *30*
Swan Lake, 34
Sweden, 34, 41
Sydney, 136; *133, 137*

Taglioni, Marie, 36, 88
Tchaikovsky, Piotr Ilich, 17, 59, 96
Tchekov, Anton, 143
Tcherepnine, Alexander, 113
Texas, 120

Tokyo, 106; *106*
Trefilova, Vera, 146
Trocadero, Paris, 102

United States of America, 41, 43–6, 49, 51–5, 59, 74, 87–96, 120–6, 130
Universal Studios, 90

Valparaiso, 101
Valse Caprice, 46, 47, *118*
Vanderbilt family, 123
Variations Grecque, 59
Vazem, Ekaterina, 41
Vienna, 64, 128
Vladimir, Grand Duke, 23
Vladimiroff, Pierre, 146; *135, 139*
Volinine, Alexander, *93, 98*

Wagner, Richard, 136
Werther, 43
West Australian, 139
Wilde, Oscar, 113
Wilhelm II, Kaiser, 82

Yokohama, 61, 105; *105*